13831725   12.95

3/81

Twayne's United States Authors Series

EDITOR OF THIS VOLUME

Kenneth Eble

University of Utah

George S. Schuyler

TUSAS 349

George S. Schuyler

GEORGE S. SCHUYLER

By MICHAEL W. PEPLOW

Lock Haven State College

TWAYNE PUBLISHERS

A DIVISION OF G. K. HALL & CO., BOSTON

Published in 1980 by Twayne Publishers,
A Division of G. K. Hall & Co.
All Rights Reserved

Printed on permanent/durable acid-free paper and bound
in the United States of America

First Printing

Library of Congress Cataloging in Publication Data

Peplow, Michael W
George S. Schuyler

(Twayne's United States authors series ; TUSAS 349)
Bibliography: p. 130-139
Includes index.
1. Schuyler, George Samuel, 1895-1977—Criticism
and interpretation. I. Title.
PS3537.C76Z83   813'.5'2   79-21363
ISBN 0-8057-7289-8

For
Cathy and Katie
and
in loving memory of Bobbie

Contents

About the Author

Michael W. Peplow, 40, teaches English and black studies courses at Lock Haven State College (central Pennsylvania), where he is chairman of the English and Philosophy Department. He co-edited *The New Negro Renaissance: An Anthology* (Holt, Rinehart, 1975) with Arthur P. Davis and *Samuel R. Delany: A Primary and Secondary Bibliography* (G. K. Hall & Co., 1980) with Robert S. Bravard. Peplow has published articles in *African Art, The Lock Haven Review, CLA Journal,* and *The Crisis* on African art and folklore, on modern African and Afro-American literatures.

Preface

George Samuel Schuyler is best known for his satiric novel on the race problem in the United States—*Black No More*. Published early in 1931, it was immediately hailed as *the satire* of the Harlem Renaissance, that literary and cultural explosion of black talent that flourished during the 1920s. Now that scholars are finally according the Harlem Renaissance the critical attention it deserves, it is time to examine its premier satirist, journalist, and essayist.

Schuyler's accomplishments are impressive:

—He wrote the first full-length satire by a black American, *Black No More*.

—He was one of our most distinguished, productive, and controversial black newspapermen for over fifty years.

—He was a muckraking journalist in the tradition of Upton Sinclair. *Slaves Today*, his second novel, is an exposé of slave traffic in Liberia in the 1920s. It was also the first African novel by a major black writer.

—He was an international correspondent of considerable stature and influence. With few exceptions, no black journalist was as widely and consistently syndicated in white and black newspapers as Schuyler.

—He wrote numerous articles, essays, and fictional pieces on America's race problem. Melvin B. Tolson called one of his essays the "greatest satire on the race problem in this country that has ever been written."

—As a critic and book reviewer, Schuyler produced several significant essays, including the often anthologized "The Negro-Art Hokum."

—He wrote the seminal history of black journalism *(Fifty Years of Negro Journalism)* and was an important spokesman on the subject of racial intermarriage.

—His autobiography, *Black and Conservative*, is not only a mine of information on most black leaders since the 1920s but a significant contribution to anti-Communist propaganda à la Westbrook Pegler.

In the process of accumulating an impressive number of "firsts," Schuyler became a figure of some controversy. His critics labeled him an "assimilationist" or Uncle Tom who expressed "the urge to whiteness" as he marched "to the sounds of a different drummer."[1] His defenders, among them W. E. B. Du Bois, Henry Lee Moon, Rayford Logan, Hugh Gloster, and Arthur P. Davis, though frequently disagreeing with him, praised his integrity and skill as a journalist and writer.[2] Rarely did they question his racial loyalty.

It is with his defenders that I side. The purpose of this study is to show that side of Schuyler which his detractors either miss or ignore. It is my conclusion that Schuyler cannot be dismissed as an assimilationist, that he was a proud race militant who consistently attacked those he felt were selling out black America.

As Schuyler's race pride was especially apparent in his early literature, I concentrate on the "literary years"—1923–1933— during which he began his career as a journalist, published his most significant essays, and produced his two novels. Except for brief comments about Schuyler's post-1933 essays and his autobiography, I leave the later Schuyler for others. This allows me to concentrate on Schuyler the satirist; it is in this area that he made his greatest contribution.

Throughout this study I quote extensively from Schuyler's work, believing that his own words will correct many of the erroneous interpretations we have inherited. In the case of typographical errors or inconsistencies, I have quietly made repairs; all his life, Schuyler waged incessant war on clumsy typesetters. One small clarification about Schuyler's language: beginning in the 1920s, he favored the term "Aframerican" instead of "Afro-American." The term is not so immediately identifiable now as it was during the Harlem Renaissance.

This book would never have been conceived or completed without the help of several people: Professors Arthur P. Davis and Marlene Mosher, who got me interested in Schuyler; the National Endowment for the Humanities, which granted me a fellowship to study at Howard University during 1973; the librarians at Howard University and Lock Haven State College, especially Marc Thomas and Robert S. Bravard, who helped me locate hundreds of documents. Also I want to thank my readers—Frank Vaughn, Bill Reich, Arthur Davis, and Elisabeth Peplow—who criticized passages that made little sense and taught me again the valuable art of revision.

Preface

My thanks also to Dr. Sylvia Bowman and Carol S. Cerino of Twayne Publishers and to Ann Peter, who typed, and retyped, this manuscript.

MICHAEL W. PEPLOW

Lock Haven State College
Lock Haven, Pennsylvania

Acknowledgments

Grateful acknowledgment is made to the following for permission to quote from works by and about George Schuyler: *The American Mercury* for passages from "Our White Folks," "Do Negroes Want to Be White?", "Black Warriors," "Memoirs of a Pearl Diver," and "Black Art"; AMS Press, Inc., New York, for passages from the reprint of *Slaves Today;* Arlington House, New Rochelle, New York, for passages from *Black and Conservative*, copyright © 1966, all rights reserved, used with permission; the College Language Association and *CLA Journal* for passages from "George Schuyler, Satirist: Rhetorical Devices in *Black No More*"; the Crisis Publishing Company for passages from "The Black *Picaro* in Schuyler's *Black No More*"; the Macmillan Publishing Company for passages from *Black No More* by George Schuyler, copyright © 1931 by The Macaulay Company and © 1970 by Macmillan Publishing Company, Inc.; *The Nation* for passages from "The Negro-Art Hokum" and "Blessed Are the Sons of Ham"; the National Urban League, Inc., for passages from "Our Greatest Gift to America"; and the Oral History Research Office, Columbia University, New York, for passages from "The Reminiscences of George S. Schuyler" in the Oral History Collection of Columbia University.

Chronology

1895   February 25: George S. Schuyler born in Providence, Rhode Island, and reared in Syracuse, New York.
1902   Educated in Syracuse public schools until 1912.
1912   Served in army through 1919. Mustered out as first lieutenant.
1923   Joined *The Messenger* staff. Assistant editor through 1928. Wrote "Shafts and Darts," a monthly column.
1924   Joined *Pittsburgh Courier* staff. Was columnist ("Views and Reviews," 1925–1966), editorial writer and associate editor (1942–1964), New York editor (1944–1960), and international correspondent (1931–1961).
1925   Began "Aframerica Today" series in the *Courier* (through 1926).
1926   "The Negro-Art Hokum" in *The Nation;* "Seldom Seen" in *The Messenger.*
1927   "Blessed are the Sons of Ham" in *The Nation;* "Our White Folks" in *The American Mercury;* "Our Greatest Gift to America" in *Ebony and Topaz.*
1928   Married Josephine Cogdell. Edited *The Illustrated Feature Section* in Chicago. "Woof" in *Harlem;* "Racial Intermarriage in the United States" in *The American Parade.*
1929   "Keeping the Negro in His Place" in *The American Mercury;* "Emancipated Woman and the Negro" in *The Modern Quarterly.*
1930   Began Young Negroes' Cooperative League. "A Negro Looks Ahead" in *The American Mercury* and *Review of Reviews;* "Traveling Jim Crow" in *The American Mercury* and *Reader's Digest;* "Black Warriors" in *The American Mercury.*
1931   *Black No More. New York Evening Post's* international correspondent to Liberia; "Slavery in Liberia" series syndicated; *Slaves Today* published. "Memoirs of a Pearl Diver" in *The American Mercury.* Philippa Schuyler born.
1932   Edited *The National News.* "Black Art" and "Black America Begins to Doubt" in *The American Mercury.* Investigated

Flood Control Project in Mississippi for NAACP (through 1933).

1934 "When Black Weds White" in *The Modern Monthly* and *Die Auslese*. Special publicity assistant to NAACP through 1935.

1937 Became business manager for *The Crisis*. Investigated labor unionism in forty industrial centers.

1943 Associate editor of *The African*.

1944 "The Caucasian Problem" in *What the Negro Wants*.

1948 *The Pittsburgh Courier*'s special correspondent to Latin America; "Racial Democracy in Latin America" series.

1949 *The Pittsburgh Courier*'s special correspondent to the West Indies; wrote "The New West Indies" series. Moderated "The Negro World" radio program for WLIB in New York.

1950 *Fifty Years of Progress in Negro Journalism*. Delegate to the Congress for Cultural Freedom (Brussels and Berlin).

1951 "The Phantom American Negro" in *Reader's Digest*.

1953 "For the Record" column syndicated by Spadea Columns, Inc., through 1962.

1956 "Do Negroes Want to be White?" in *The American Mercury*.

1958 *The Pittsburgh Courier*'s special correspondent to West Africa and the Dominican Republic.

1959 "Krushchev's African Foothold" in *The American Mercury*.

1960 *The Pittsburgh Courier*'s special correspondent to Nigeria. Interviewed for Oral History Collection at Columbia University.

1961 Probably joined the John Birch Society; began to write for the Society's *American Opinion*. *The Pittsburgh Courier*'s special correspondent to then-Portuguese Africa.

1964 Nominated by New York Conservative Party to run against Adam Clayton Powell. Began regular contributions to the *Manchester* (New Hampshire) *Union Leader* with article criticizing Martin Luther King.

1965 Began to contribute regularly to the North American Newspaper Alliance. Was attacked editorially in *The Crisis*.

1966 Stopped writing "Views and Reviews" column and left *The Pittsburgh Courier*. Published *Black and Conservative*.

1967 Became analysis editor and film reviewer for *Review of the News* and literary editor ("The Literary Line") for *Manchester Union Leader*. May 9: Philippa Schuyler killed in Viet Nam.

1968 Received American Legion Award.

Chronology

1969 Received Citation from Catholic War Veterans. May 2: Josephine Schuyler died.
1972 Received Freedoms Foundation Award at Valley Forge.
1973 "Malcolm X: Better to Memorialize Benedict Arnold" in *American Opinion*.
1977 August 31: George S. Schuyler died at New York Hospital.

CHAPTER 1

The Lonely Iconoclast: A Biography

I have always said and written just what I thought without apologies to anyone," wrote George Schuyler in 1934 in a letter to the American Worker's Party.[1] "Whatever I think is wrong, I shall continue to attack. Whatever is right, I shall continue to laud. . . . I have always been more concerned with being true to myself than to any group. . . . I shall continue to pursue this somewhat lonely and iconoclastic course" (223).

Schuyler lived by those words. Thirty-two years later, in his autobiography *Black and Conservative,* he proudly quoted them. And nearly ten years later, when I interviewed him in New York, he described himself as a career-long iconoclast.

I first met George Schuyler in October 1973, and I interviewed him both in person and by telephone over the next two years.[2] The first time we met, I approached Schuyler with trepidation; not only had he a reputation for being an expert interviewer who might laugh at my clumsy questions, but he was also known as a blunt man with a wicked sense of humor. Carefully I asked my first question: Was Schuyler still a lonely iconoclast?

"Am I an iconoclast? Sure! Lonely? Hell no! I've got lots of friends."

But in his last years Schuyler did not have many friends. First his daughter and then his wife died tragically. One black organization after another either turned on him, labeling him an Uncle Tom, or decided to ignore him completely. His far-to-the-right comments on Martin Luther King, Malcolm X, and the Civil Rights movement alienated a new generation of black leaders in the mid-1960s. His literary accomplishments were forgotten. By 1975, no matter how defiantly he answered my questions, Schuyler was alone. Two years later he died alone.

There were a few who recalled Schuyler's wit and bluntness when asked by the *New York Times* for statements for an obituary. John

17

Henrik Clarke, the noted black historian, recalled that "I used to
tell people that George got up in the morning, waited to see which
way the world was turning, then struck out in the opposite direc-
tion." Clarke concluded that Schuyler "was a rebel who enjoyed
playing that role."[3]
    The story of how George Schuyler became a rebel, and why he
enjoyed being one, is fascinating.

I   *The Formative Years: 1895–1919*

    To understand Schuyler, it's necessary to realize at the outset that
he was born a black Yankee, reared in a small, mostly white
community, and trained from the earliest years in traditional Yankee
virtues like self-discipline, independence, thrift, and industry. A
sort of black Horatio Alger, Schuyler could well have become one
of the black intellectuals whom he grew to distrust and against
whom he directed much of his best satire.
    Schuyler's great grandfather was a freed black man who served
under (white) General Philip Schuyler during the Revolutionary
War. His great-grandmother, who came from Madagascar, married
a white sea captain; his grandmother and mother were born and
reared in New York City. Schuyler's parents "boasted of having
been free as far back as any of them [the family] could . . .
remember, and they haughtily looked down upon those who had
been born in servitude. They neither cherished nor sang slave
songs" (3–4).
    Although born in Providence, Rhode Island, Schuyler was taken
to the family home in Syracuse, New York, before he was a year old.
His father died in 1898, and his mother married again.
    Young Schuyler was exposed to literature in general and to black
history and literature in particular. From a home library of one
hundred books, he chose works like *The Black Phalanx,* an early
favorite, which taught him about those "Negro soldiers and sailors
who had fought in all our wars." This "was a fascinating revelation,
and no colored child could harbor any feeling of inferiority after-
ward. It was even more impressive to know that many such
background books were written by colored people" (13). Schuyler's
mother cultivated his interest in "such outstanding . . . people as
Bishop Alexander Crummel, Booker T. Washington, Frederick
Douglass, . . . and Harriet Tubman" (18). Schuyler later claimed
that "I came up in an atmosphere where there were plenty of books

and where the people knew the background of the Negro. My first interest in Negro history and background came right there at home. . . ."[4] Given his early awareness of and pride in his black heritage, it is not surprising that Schuyler later criticized Negroes who claimed "exotic" instead of black blood: "I am one of the . . . sable hue who boast no Indian or Caucasian blood. . . . My folks have just been free black citizens of New York State for the last one-hundred and twenty-five years."[5]

Schuyler attended local grammar and high schools until he was seventeen, then dropped out to enlist in the army. He served from 1912 to 1919. As a member of the famed Twenty-Fifth U.S. Infantry, a black outfit, Schuyler either visited or served in Seattle, Hawaii, Japan, the Philippines, and China. He became a soldier's soldier during those years yet still meshed well with fellow troops; indeed, he prided himself on being able to gamble, drink, wench, fight, and hustle officers as well as any soldier. Later he immortalized his wartime adventures in "Woof" and "Black Warriors" and in *Black and Conservative*.

Schuyler found time during the army years to develop his journalistic skills and to polish his satire. Satire apparently came naturally to Schuyler. At the age of ten, he "composed a verse lampooning an obnoxious school-teacher"; four years later he "did a parody on Macaulay's 'Horatius,' aimed at school authorities.[6] In Hawaii, he wrote satirical sketches for *The Service*. At about the same time, "the regimental commander suppressed a daily type-written journal of news and rather biting comment, *The Daily Dope*, which I edited."[7] During these same years, he taught classes in English and geography for his fellow soldiers and wrote occasional pieces for Honolulu daily newspapers.

What was to become a fighting black militantism combined with a relish for the absurd manifested itself in an incident that Schuyler described first in "Black Warriors" (see Chapter 4) and later in his autobiography. He and four enlisted men entered a Seattle bar that was hostile to black customers. The bartender "grimly set the drinks in front of us, . . . then took the five empty glasses and one by one smashed them on the floor, as we watched with mounting rage." Just as grimly the men ordered another round. The same thing happened. So Schuyler said: "Give us five beers. . . The beer glasses cost more." Again the same result—and the charade continued until the bartender ordered the men to leave. But soon they returned—with forty black soldiers:

We lined up and put our feet on the brass rail.
The bartender was thunderstruck.
"What do you people want?" he asked weakly.
"Beer all round," I ordered grandly, ringing a five-dollar gold piece on the bar.
The bartender scratched his head and grinned sheepishly and drew the foaming brew. We tossed it off, slamming the goblets down on the bar, and waited.
"You boys win," the bartender conceded. "Have one on the house!"

Schuyler concludes: "At any rate we had staged the first stand-in and won" (41–43).

II Hobo and Journalist During the Harlem Renaissance: 1919–1924

Discharged in 1919 as a first lieutenant, Schuyler took a temporary civil service position, then a series of menial jobs which gave him rich material for later articles and columns. In New York City, he worked variously as a porter, printer's messenger, and dishwasher. Returning briefly to Syracuse in 1922, he founded a housecleaning business, then became a hod-carrier and building laborer and joined a union in 1922. While in Syracuse he also joined the Socialist Party of America.

After he returned to New York during the winter of 1922–1923, he lived with a picturesque group of hobos in a Bowery flophouse. "The folk farthest down" were immortalized in "Hobohemia" for *The Messenger,* in "Memoirs of a Pearl Diver" for *The American Mercury,* and in various columns.[8] Later Schuyler noted that the "common folk" were always the best source of information on what it was like to live in any community, be it small Southern town, large Northern metropolis, or Liberian bush.[9]

New York and especially Harlem was a fascinating place in the 1920s for an aspiring black journalist. It was the beginning of the Harlem Renaissance, which produced a wealth of literature by those young authors whom Dr. Alain Locke called the New Negroes (as opposed to older Booker T. Washington–oriented Negroes) that set forth in uncompromising terms a new black militancy.[10] W.E.B. Du Bois, co-founder of the NAACP and editor of its house organ, *The Crisis,* was one of the leaders of the age. Another was Locke himself, who compiled the most significant anthology of New Negro literature—*The New Negro* (1925). Still another was Eugene

Kinckle Jones, a member of the National Urban League and editor of *Opportunity*, the league's monthly publication. Others included A. Philip Randolph and Chandler Owen, the founders of the "radical" socialist journal, *The Messenger*—the men who discovered Schuyler. These men not only campaigned for immediate manhood rights but featured in the pages of their newspapers and magazines a host of young New Negroes (all of whom Schuyler knew well), including Langston Hughes, Countee Cullen, Claude McKay, Arna Bontemps, Jean Toomer, Jessie Fauset, Zora Neale Hurston, and Anne Spencer.

The renaissance was a rebirth of the black literary impetus begun twenty or so years earlier which culminated in the work of Charles W. Chesnutt and Paul Laurence Dunbar. The era when the Negro was "in vogue," according to Langston Hughes,[11] lasted from the end of World War I until the Depression. Slumming whites went uptown to experience the exotic-erotic "primitivism" of Harlem nightclubs. White publications such as *The Nation* and *The American Mercury* enthusiastically solicited literature by and about Negro Americans. And serious white authors—Eugene O'Neill and Ridgley Torrence—worked with black authors to counteract still popular stereotypes of the Negro (see Chapter 2).

Historians have demonstrated that the Harlem Renaissance was made possible in large measure by the overall euphoria that affected America after the world "had been made safe for democracy" during World War I. The larger American scene in the 1920s is now associated with words and phrases like "the roaring twenties," "prohibition," "flappers," "the jazz age," and "speakeasies." This euphoria (which included a fascination with the Negro American) suddenly and dramatically collapsed in 1929.

By 1923, Schuyler was ready to participate in the Harlem Renaissance. He began publishing pieces supporting the new "radical" ideas of immediate manhood rights, equal consideration before the law, and an end to lynchings, Jim Crow, and second class citizenship. At the same time, he lived in the midst of what he later described as the golden age of American satire.[12] His style shows the influence of fellow iconoclasts (H. L. Mencken was a personal friend), parodists (Corey Ford, Don Marquis, Louis Untermeyer, Robert Benchley, George Ade), and social satirists (George Bernard Shaw, Will Rogers, Sherwood Anderson, Sinclair Lewis). He read (and later published in) *The American Mercury, The Nation,* and other forward-looking publications. Inevitably he sharpened a style already influenced by Juvenal, Horace, Swift, Shaw, Twain, and Anatole France (*Penguin Island*, Schuyler once told me, had a profound influence on him). Soon, Schuyler emerged as one of the major New Negro satirists (Wallace Thurman and Rudolph Fisher were two others), one of *les enfants terribles* who attacked the excesses of the Harlem Renaissance, while Mencken, Lardner, Lewis, and Rogers ridiculed the smugness of white America.

In 1923, his education in the Bowery complete, Schuyler joined the staff of *The Messenger*. Soon he became a contributing editor, one of "those honest, serious, brilliant, and bold spirits who dare with tongue and pen, to proclaim the shortcomings of the existing social order and . . . seek to guide the tortured and exploited masses to a better world."[13] In June 1923 Schuyler's delightful "Hobohemia" appeared; hobos, said Schuyler, are "the best people on earth," "the most open-hearted people the writer has ever met"; among them, racial prejudice is "almost completely non-existent." They are the "rebels against the shackles of society" and therefore superior to "the snobs."[14]

His first regular satirical column, "Shafts and Darts: A Page of Calumny and Satire," began in *The Messenger* the following month. At times he collaborated with Theophilus Lewis, another black satirist. Whether he attacked individuals (Marcus Garvey and other "race leaders" who "misled" the common man) or groups (the Ku Klux Klan, Christian missionaries, government officials, hair-straightening and skin-whitening blacks), Schuyler was always scathing. Typically, in the early columns he would quote a news story that had absurd ramifications, then comment, bitingly and punningly, on its significance for the average black man. As Schuyler's skill developed, his entries became longer and better developed. Some of his "Aframerican Fables" approached mature satire. For several months Schuyler awarded "the grand monthly . . . handsomely embossed and beautifully lacquered dill pickle" to some "notable white or black American who had recently said or done something particularly asinine."[15] He enjoyed commenting on news stories, especially when he could needle idiots: " 'Boy Choir Singer, Son of Minister, Admits Hold-Ups.' . . . Like father, like son!"[16]

An early piece, written in league with Lewis, explains his *modus operandi*:

[Our] intention is . . . to slur, lampoon, damn and occasionally praise anybody or anything in the known universe, not excepting the President of

the immortals. . . . Furthermore [we] make no effort to conceal the fact
that [our] dominant motive is a malicious one and that our paragraphs of
praise shall be few and far between, while [we] go to greater lengths to
discover and expose the imbecilities, knavery and pathological virtues of
[our] fellowman. . . . If any considerable body of Americans were intelligent in the human sense, or even civilized, . . . their manly and dignified
behavior would be copied. . . . It pains this pair of misanthropes even to
think of such a state of affairs, and they fervently hope their excursions into
morbid humor will not be confused with the crusade of benevolent killjoys
to change America *puissant,* Philistine and gullible to America sophisti-
cated, civilized and sane.[17]

This is as concise a statement of Schuyler's satiric pose as exists.
Frequently, he posed as a misanthrope. He appeared to see only
stupidity and vice on every side. It was his duty—his sacred
obligation—to expose them. A blunt man of the people, he was
literally forced to attack, no matter how politically touchy, obscene,
or even "low" his subject matter and tone. Cutting humor was the
weapon with which he ridiculed foolishness and vice.

Schuyler's satire soon found space in other publications. In 1924,
he started "This Simian World" in *The Pittsburgh Courier,* for many
years the leading black weekly in America. In one sketch Schuyler
pretends to interview the "dean of the Simians" at the zoo; the ape
informs him that "it is evident that humanity descended because it
has never shown any evidence of ascending."[18] This bleak vision of
man is developed in a longer sketch in his next series of columns for
The Pittsburgh Courier, "Thrusts and Lunges." In one Schuyler
explained why Martians had not contacted earthlings; coinciden-
tally, he provided an early list of his major adversaries:

The first thing they [the Martians] discovered was that the so-called human
race was underdeveloped. . . . [because] of such curious phenomena as the
enforcement of prohibition, conventions of fraternal organizations, parades
of [Garvey's] U.N.I.A., the mendacity of American college presidents, a
lynching, a Billy Sunday revival and an annual election to determine which
lawyers would draw salaries without working for the next two or six years.
In addition . . . they were regaled by the sight of black folks hunting bleach
and white folks hunting sunburn; blacks straightening their curly hair and
whites curling their straight hair; Communists planning a "boring from
within" expedition at a "secret" meeting . . . , and a contingent of the Ku
Klux Klan appealing for freedom of speech and assembly in an Irish
community. They saw . . . the Euro-Americans up in arms over miscegenation, while five million mulattoes looked on; . . . Of course, the civilized

Martians laughed until they cried at the spectacle, and immediately concluded that *the insane asylum of the universe* had been discovered (my
italics).[19]

But Schuyler did not just write satire. In more serious pieces, his
love of race and pride in black heroes emerged. By May 1924, he
was writing *Messenger* articles on prominent black Americans,
including Madame Walker, Mortimer Harris (a realtor), and John A.
Lankford (an architect). About the same time, Schuyler urged J. A.
Rogers, the noted black historian, to write "a monthly article on
great men and women in Negro history," thus "anticipating the rash
of such articles and books in the 1960s" (159). In *The Pittsburgh
Courier*, he argued that monuments should be raised in the United
States "commemorating the achievements, sacrifices and tribula-
tions of Sojourner Truth, Denmark Vesey, Paul Laurence Dunbar
. . . [and] Frederick Douglass."[20] Two months later he published a
significant article, "Speaking of Monuments and History," in which
he recommended raising edifices to "great Negro men and women."
Instead of memorializing black soldiers who fought in white wars,
"as proposed by several race leaders," monuments should be
erected that will "impress on the minds of the white and black
citizens the fact that occasionally we have been loyal to OUR-
SELVES." "Between 1526 and 1859," Schuyler notes, "there were
nearly forty insurrections and conspiracies organized by our en-
slaved forefathers and their friends." They should be immortalized
because "they organized and often shed their blood and gave their
lives on the altar of liberty—FOR THEMSELVES." Schuyler then
lists a number of black Americans, Africans, and Europeans who
should be so honored, including Cato, Gabriel, Denmark Vesey,
Nat Turner, Toussaint L'Ouverture, Chaka, Ira Aldridge,
Coleridge-Taylor, Juan Latino, Antar, Pushkin, Alexander Dumas,
Phillis Wheatley, Paul Laurence Dunbar, Estevanico, Harriet
Tubman, and Sojourner Truth.[21]

III   *National and International Correspondent: 1924–1933*

By 1924 Schuyler was writing columns and occasional pieces for
both *The Messenger* and *The Pittsburgh Courier*. His longest
running column, "Views and Reviews," began to appear in *The
Courier* in October. His first major assignment involved touring
over two hundred Southern communities to prepare a series on
"Aframerica Today", which began to appear November 14, 1925.

One article, "Memphis—Cotton Metropolis," is typical of his maturing style, revealing his knowledge of the effectiveness of a strong opening, local color, vivid detail, and language that makes the reader feel he was standing in Memphis with Schuyler. His opening paragraph approaches poetry:

Memphis, gateway to the cotton belt. Memphis, seventh heaven of white and black Mississippians. Memphis, murder mart *per excellence*. . . . Air redolent with sinister expectancy. Memphis, bustling metropolis with massive buildings, well-paved streets, beautiful public structures . . . and jim crow bars. . . . Memphis, home of . . . the Blues. Here is Beale Street: pawn shops . . . barbecue joints . . . bootleg emporiums . . . restaurants . . . drug stores . . . camouflaged bordellos . . . Negro banks . . . big Negro insurance offices . . . doctors . . . gamblers . . . barber shops . . . pimps . . . dentists . . . prostitutes . . . boisterous laughter . . . the tinkle of a piano . . . the rattle of a street car . . . a savage oath . . . a shot![22]

When Schuyler finished his Southern tour and resumed his duties at *The Messenger* and *The Pittsburgh Courier*, his career had been launched. A month before he returned, *The Nation* published "The Negro-Art Hokum," an article which presented one aspect of a very complex critical discussion during the Harlem Renaissance (see Chapter 2). He was paid fifteen dollars for the now famous piece.[23] Schuyler soon became assistant editor for *The Messenger* and chief editorial writer for *The Pittsburgh Courier*. Later in 1926, his "Southern Snapshots" was published in Mike Gold's *The New Masses* and reprinted in part in *El Sol*, a Mexico City Communist publication. By the end of the year, Schuyler was appointed managing editor of *The Messenger*.

In March 1927, "Blessed Are the Sons of Ham" was published in *The Nation*. In December, "Our White Folks," a piece personally solicited by H. L. Menchen, appeared in the influential *The American Mercury*. *Ebony and Topaz*, an anthology published by the National Urban League in 1927, included "Our Greatest Gift to America," another of Schuyler's best pieces. It was reprinted in 1929 in V. F. Calverton's *Anthology of American Negro Literature*.

In January 1928, the thirty-two year old Schuyler, until then a confirmed bachelor, married a white Texas ex-model, Josephine Cogdell.[24] Schuyler and his bride soon moved to Chicago so he could edit *The Illustrated Feature Section*, a weekly magazine insert for black newspapers. By July *The Messenger* had collapsed, but Schuyler continued to write for *The Pittsburgh Courier* as well as producing several pieces for other publications. His much-admired

"Woof" appeared in the single issue of *Harlem*, a renaissance magazine. *The American Parade* published "Racial Intermarriage in the United States," a monograph later republished in the Little Blue Book series. *The American Mercury* featured "Keeping the Negro in His Place" in August, and V. F. Calverton, the man who, according to Schuyler, later urged him to write *Black No More*, featured "Emancipated Woman and the Negro" in *The Modern Quarterly*.

The next three years were extraordinarily productive ones. While working for *The Pittsburgh Courier*, Schuyler also wrote "A Negro Looks Ahead" (February 1930), "Travelling Jim Crow" (August 1930), "Black Warriors" (November 1930), "Memoirs of a Pearl Diver" (April 1931), "Black America Begins to Doubt" (April 1932), and "Black Art" (November 1932) for *The American Mercury*. "Travelling Jim Crow" appeared in truncated form in the infant *Reader's Digest* in 1930. *Black No More*, his first novel, was published in January 1931, at the same time that the author was forming his dreamed of—and doomed—Young Negroes' Cooperative League.[25] In the same month, Schuyler set sail for Great Britain, apparently in order to study English cooperative wholesale societies. In fact, though he spent a few weeks in Britain, Schuyler was on an even more important mission: hired as a secret foreign correspondent by George Palmer Putnam, the publisher, and Julian Mason, editor of *The New York Evening Post*, Schuyler was sent to investigate recent, sensational stories about Liberia's modern slave trade. Returning in May 1931, Schuyler published a series of controversial articles on Liberia in *The Washington Post, The New York Evening News, The Philadelphia Ledger*, and *The Pittsburgh Courier* (see Chapter 4). At the end of the year, Schuyler's second novel, *Slaves Today*, was published by Brewer, Warren and Putnam.

In 1932, Schuyler continued his hectic pace. Undertaking a series of lectures on his cooperative league and on Liberia, he also resigned from *The Pittsburgh Courier* to edit a Harlem weekly, *The National News: The News Magazine of Colored America* (February-September). His book reviews appeared in *Opportunity*, his articles in *The American Mercury, The Crisis*, and *The Forum*. He participated in a national Negro forum on station WEVD. By the end of 1932, he was again on secret assignment, this time with the young Roy Wilkins, for the NAACP's *Crisis*. The two men were assigned to investigate labor conditions on the Mississippi Flood

Control Project. Schuyler was arrested in Vicksburg on what turned
out to be a case of mistaken identity.

"My room was not broken into, but they beat on the door and
came in . . . with pistols drawn . . . and took me to the police
station . . . [and] kept me overnight," recollected Schuyler in
"Reminiscences." The police, in fact, were searching for a black
criminal who looked something like Schuyler. They decided the
author might be their man and so threw him into jail for the night.
The next morning, "they took $30 and a Shaeffer lifetime pen off of
me . . . and told me to get out of Mississippi and not come
back. . . ."[26] Fortunately Schuyler had hidden $25 in the toe of his
shoe before the arrest, which the police did not find.

Although at the height of his fame and skill, Schuyler was
beginning to suffer setbacks by 1933. After his arrest, he returned to
New York to learn that his cooperative league had produced angry
rejoinders from the staid Colored Merchants Association and from
its sister organization, the National Negro Business League. Instead
of being diplomatic, Schuyler quickly attacked these organizations.
His independent venture, *The National News*, died almost before it
got started. The articles on Liberia were condemned by Garveyites,
missionaries, and those who felt Schuyler had been duped by a
white publishing company. His slashing attack on the Negro church,
"Black America Begins to Doubt," drew heavy criticism; even
though Schuyler had always professed atheism, his essay was too
overstated, too venomous, and in some places untrue.

IV   The Later Years: 1934–1977

Schuyler wrote in *Black and Conservative:* "I devoted my attention to the Communist Conspiracy" after the publication of *Slaves
Today*" (186). In "Reminiscences" he insisted that as early as 1924
he had "dumped" socialism "overboard."[27] In both cases he pre-
dated his anti-Communist crusade. There is no evidence of any
new-found conservatism in *Black No More* or in his columns in *The
Pittsburgh Courier*. Although he seemed to drift somewhat towards
anti-Communism in his comments on the celebrated Scottsboro
case in the 1930s,[28] he did not fully commit himself to the cause
until 1939, the year he published "Negroes Reject Communism" in
The American Mercury. Indeed, according to some, Schuyler's

columns did not become rabidly anti-Communist until the McCarthy years.[29]

But during those same years, Schuyler did remain consistently dedicated to the race issue. Between 1934 and 1944 he was active in the National Association for the Advancement of Colored People (NAACP), especially as the organization's business manager from 1937 to 1944. He also put in time with the association's publicity department. During these years he wrote articles such as "Scripture for Lynchers," "Reflections on Negro Leadership," "Battering Down The Barriers of Prejudice," and "Do Negroes Want to be White?" He continued to write about Liberia, producing "Uncle Sam's Black Step-Child," "Woman Palaver," "The Lord's Work," and "Monrovia Mooches On." He also continued to review books ("*Not* Gone With The Wind" is especially ferocious).

During the same years and well into the 1960s Schuyler continued to enjoy prominence as a national and international correspondent. In 1937 he investigated the role of black workers in the industrial labor union drive, and in 1938 he investigated Negro labor racketeers in Chicago (at one point he had an eyeball-to-eyeball confrontation with a black mobster that probably aged him ten years[30]). In 1943 he became associate editor of *The African* and thereafter published monthly columns such as "Things of No Importance" and "It Happened in Africa." In 1944 he became New York editor of *The Pittsburgh Courier*. After World War II he participated in a *Negro Digest* (later *Black World*) symposium, "Should Negroes in the South Migrate North?" and published one of his better-known satiric essays, "The Caucasian Problem," in Rayford Logan's *What the Negro Wants*. For *The Pittsburgh Courier*, Schuyler served as special correspondent to Latin America ("Racial Democracy in Latin America" appeared in 1949). In December 1949 he began a weekly radio program, "The Negro World," for WLIB in New York. During June of the following year, he was the U.S. delegate to the Berlin and Brussels meetings of the Congress for Cultural Freedom, an anti-Communist seminar at which he delivered "The Negro Question Without Propaganda," which was subsequently read into the U.S. Congressional Record (1950). In that same year his *Fifty Years of Progress in Negro Journalism* was published in Pittsburgh. In July 1951 *Reader's Digest* carried his second contribution, "The Phantom American Negro," and in November he participated in a television symposium, "Are We Close to Solving Our Race Problem?"

By 1960, however, he had begun to have trouble with the management at *The Pittsburgh Courier;* he was soon replaced as the New York editor of that publication. That same year, he was interviewed for the Columbia Oral History series. Soon he decided to join the John Birch Society (he dates it rather vaguely as "sometime in the early 1960s"). The following year he was *The Pittsburgh Courier's* correspondent to Portuguese Africa and began writing for *American Opinion*, a John Birch monthly published in Massachusetts. In 1964 he became active in politics, accepting the New York State Conservative Party's nomination to run against Adam Clayton Powell in the 18th (Harlem) District—a race which he lost. In 1964 his conflict with *The Pittsburgh Courier* became more intense after he wrote an article criticizing the awarding of the Nobel prize for peace to Martin Luther King. *The Pittsburgh Courier* refused to publish the piece, so Schuyler ceased most of his *Courier* activities. The King article, incidentally, was published November 10, 1964 in William Loeb's *Manchester Union Leader.* The following year, Schuyler contributed an article attacking the Watts rioters and was quickly and openly criticized in a *Crisis* editorial. In 1966, *Black and Conservative* was published by Arlington House. The same year Schuyler finally left *The Pittsburgh Courier* completely, joined William Loeb's staff, and began writing for the *Review of the News*, a John Birch weekly published in Belmont, Massachusetts.

The incidents surrounding Schuyler's leaving *The Pittsburgh Courier* are not at all clear. *The Pittsburgh Courier* refused to answer my queries about Schuyler. Some outside sources argue that Schuyler was fired for columns such as the one on Martin Luther King. Schuyler told me in no uncertain terms, "I severed connections with the *Courier* in 1966 and went immediately to the *Manchester Union Leader.* . . . When I get through with something, I just go on to something else. I was not fired. . . . The paper folded and they [decided] to set up a new establishment."

In 1967 Philippa Schuyler was killed while covering the war in Viet Nam for Loeb's newspaper. Two years later Josephine, Schuyler's wife, died, and Schuyler was left alone in his Harlem apartment overflowing with *objets d'art* acquired during a lifetime of travel. Until the end he remained "out of step" with mainstream black America, very much the "lonely iconoclast." When he died August 31, 1977 in New York Hospital, he was 82 years old.

Though Schuyler prided himself in his tough realism, others

noted additional qualities. William Loeb, for example, wrote me a long letter describing George Schuyler. Here's an excerpt:

The day of Philippa's funeral saw George as . . . [a] composed man. Whatever he felt inside he knew that a gentleman doesn't bare [his feelings] to the rest of the world. . . . Barely a year later [sic], George lost his wife. So, that brave old gentleman is alone, without loved ones to care [for him] as he watches the world going mad. He lives in that apartment, doing the best he can and not becoming bitter but battling on.[31]

"My impression of George," concluded Loeb, "is one of a greatly balanced individual whose judgment and dedication and devotion to principle is so strong that he has *no intention of being swayed by praise or criticism*" (my italics).[32] An iconoclast. Lonely, perhaps, but a man we should listen to. Rayford Logan said in 1973 that Schuyler "could cut deeply and sometimes unfairly, but he was always interesting to read."[33] Henry Lee Moon, a former editor of *The Crisis*, said that Schuyler "was an iconoclast. He was self-educated, but well educated. He was always worth reading. I often disagree with him. . . . He was not run-of-the-mill. Schuyler was creative."[34]

All of these comments help us to understand this man, but one of Schuyler's last comments to me, made in a light-hearted moment, typified the man for me: "I've had a lot of fun watching the passing scene. . . ."[35]

CHAPTER 2

Literary Criticism: Young Radical or Lampblacked Anglo-Saxon?

IN 1931, W. E. B. DuBois wrote: "I have watched the procession of young radicals since before the world war with lack-luster eyes, . . . always asking myself: are they going to be willing to pay the price? . . . George Schuyler, so far, is talking things that most people do not want to hear. . . . One has to read what he says, whether he agrees with it or not."[1]

From the beginning, Schuyler delighted in saying things that people did not want to hear. In "The Negro-Art Hokum," for example, he wrote that "the Aframerican is merely a lampblacked Anglo-Saxon." Such a statement smacked of "the urge to whiteness" or assimilationism that Schuyler's critics cite to prove his race disloyalty.[2] What the critics often do not take into account is the temper of the times in which Schuyler wrote these words. So, in order to understand "The Negro-Art Hokum," we need first to examine the critical debate of the 1920s.

I   The Critical Debate of the Harlem Renaissance

In the 1920s, "The Negro-Art Hokum" was not nearly as heretical a document as it seems now. It was Schuyler's contribution to an ongoing critical debate that involved most of the major black, and white, writers of the renaissance.[3]

One aspect of the debate was the issue of whether a black author should write *black* or as an American who *happens* to be black. By extension, Is the black writer to project racial themes or universal ones? William Stanley Braithwaite, a nationally known black critic, wrote poetry in which there was no allusion at all to race ("raceless literature"), and he advised Claude McKay to avoid racial themes as well. Countee Cullen said: "As heretical as it may sound, there is

31

the probability that Negro poets, dependent as they are on the English language, may have more to gain from the rich background of English and American poetry than from any nebulous atavistic yearnings towards an African inheritance."[4] There was a school of "genteel literature" during the Harlem Renaissance, in opposition to the "street-life" literature represented by, say, Claude McKay, that emphasized either the "raceless" or the "best-foot-forward" themes. The issue of a "black" versus a "universal" literature became so intense that in the same year "The Negro-Art Hokum" appeared, *The Crisis* published a symposium on "The Negro in Art: How Shall He Be Portrayed?" It attracted responses from several major black and many white authors concerned with the "race question."

That there was a definite middle class, "genteel," even "assimilationist" tendency in the Harlem Renaissance is too often ignored by critics searching for the seeds of a unified modern black aesthetic in the 1920s. Yet, no matter what their critical stance, most writers did concentrate on race themes whether in the protest, race pride, African heritage, or "nigger heaven" traditions.[5] (Schuyler followed suit: all of his major literature was devoted to the race issue.)

The critical debate of the Harlem Renaissance, it seems to me, was more about what black writers would have liked to have seen written under ideal conditions. Perhaps the most famous critical statement of the period came from Langston Hughes in his "response" to Schuyler, entitled "The Negro Artist and the Racial Mountain."[6] After criticizing a hypothetical "young Negro poet" for wanting to write "like a white poet" instead of "being himself," Hughes said:

We younger Negro artists . . . now intend to express our individual dark-skinned selves without fear or shame. If white people are pleased we are glad. If they are not, it doesn't matter. . . . If colored people are pleased we are glad. If they are not, their displeasure doesn't matter either. We build our temples for tomorrow, strong as we know how, and we stand on top of the mountain, free within ourselves.[7]

Interpretation of this famous passage, I believe, depends on whether we stress "individual" or "dark-skinned." Is Hughes saying that the black writer should be an individualist even if this might mean he doesn't write black? Or is he saying that the author's primary duty is to stress his "dark-skinned heritage? If we assume the latter, then Hughes was probably thinking in terms of art as propaganda as well as of a black aesthetic for the 1920s. Whatever the answers, the critical debate never was resolved during the Harlem Renaissance. It was bequeathed to the new black writers and critics of the 1960s and 1970s. There is still disagreement about the role of the black artist in a white-dominated society.

Important as the critical debate of the 1920s was in its own right, we must also realize that it was an extension of an old political debate. Should the New Negro espouse the conservative, accommodationist philosophy of Booker T. Washington and his successors? Or should he follow the militant demand, as defined by men like Du Bois, for immediate social, political, and cultural equality? The new militancy gained the upper hand during the 1920s, but it was complicated by yet another factor: just how militant should the New Negro be? On a scale ranging from total accommodationism (Booker T. Washington) to total separatism (Marcus Garvey), most of the New Negroes accepted the "middle stance" prescribed by the NAACP, the National Urban League, the Brotherhood of Sleeping Car Porters, and so forth. Like the early Du Bois, Alain Locke, Eugene Kinckle Jones, and A. Philip Randolph, Schuyler avoided the extremes. He was a Du Boisian "radical" well within the Harlem Renaissance mainstream of the 1920s. [8]

The political issue is important because in the 1920s the ghost of accommodationism had not yet been fully laid to rest. Literature featuring traditional stereotyped white clichés of a naturally inferior, childlike Negro was popular. Many black authors and critics found themselves compelled to fight the old battle. Kelly Miller had fired an opening salvo in 1905 with his "Open Letter" to Thomas Dixon. Du Bois and others followed suit in "The Niagara Statement" (1905) and "The Objectives of the NAACP" (1910). So did Alain Locke in "The New Negro." And so did Schuyler in "The Negro-Art Hokum."

II *Schuyler's Early Critical Statements*

From 1923 on, Schuyler wrote reviews that reveal how race conscious he really was. Although sometimes disagreeing with the philosophies of black authors, he nevertheless wrote positive reviews if they met certain Schuylerian requirements: a good work, he believed, must be true to life, grounded in fact, realistic; it must be readable and appeal to the average man as opposed to the "snobboc-racy"; finally, it must truly reflect the black experience.

In 1924, for example, he wrote that Walter White's *The Fire in the Flint*, was "creative," "an exceptionally fine piece of work," "a wonderful mine of information" about the South, "absolutely true and faithful." The characters are "human beings," not types, and the setting "is as well drawn as anything of its kind in literature."[9]

Du Bois, a man Schuyler frequently criticized, was warmly praised in 1924 for *The Gift of Black Folk*. Du Bois is "our greatest Aframerican literatus," and *The Gift of Black Folk* works hard to "reverse" the Negro inferiority complex: "I have always felt that a knowledge of the history and achievements of the Negro in America and elsewhere would do much to dispel [the] illusion of inferiority." The Aframerican must realize that the Negro "was probably the factor in making the United States what it is today," that black women "were pioneers actively and passively," that Negro art, literature, music, and religious spirit "contributed largely toward the gradual emancipation of America from the deadening influence of puritanical ethics." Du Bois' work fills "the breast of every black man, woman and child with a just pride in the fact that they are Negroes."[10]

Schuyler was also quick to attack black writers who in one way or another "betrayed" the race. He faulted Kelly Miller's *The Everlasting Stain*, for being a "middle-of-the-road," antiradical work permeated by a "Tuskegee mentality." He "repudiates . . . social equality" while "loudly advertising the Negro's loyalty, meakness, and forgiving nature." Worst of all he "ballyhoos for the white man's burden."[11]

In succeeding columns, Schuyler praised works by James Weldon Johnson, J. A. Rogers, and two satirists—Eugene Huffman and Wallace Thurman.[12] But Schuyler especially praised Langston Hughes' *Not Without Laughter*, "*the* novel of Negro life" as far as Schuyler was concerned: "More than a novel, it is a social docu-ment, an epic on the sable lowly that white America looks down upon. Here we have the suffering, the pleasures, the loves and hates, the hopes, aspirations and frustrations of Negro Proletarians." For "the ordinary Negro reader," the novel "arouses the memories of youth, of yesterday and today." Concludes Schuyler: "*I know* the people in this novel, every one of them. They are in a hundred little ghettos. . . . The *people* are *real* and their impact is *real*."[13]

The publication of "The Negro-Art Hokum" in 1926 caused a stir among the intellectuals of the Harlem Renaissance. Schuyler later said that he submitted the article before he went on his Southern tour and that the editor of *The Nation* refused to publish it for over a year, during which time she sent it around to various black leaders for their reaction; she finally published the article, but followed it up in the next issue with Langston Hughes' essay. If this is the case, then Schuyler was probably shabbily treated.[14]

In essence, Schuyler's was the standard leftist position (he was still a socialist in 1926) of the 1920's—namely, that all men are brothers under the skin, that art is more a product of environment than genetics, and that black literature should avoid being "peculiar" (i.e., "inferior") and should stay within the mainstream. At the same time, as mentioned earlier, Schuyler was fighting the old battle against white stereotyping of "comical" or "brute niggers" à la Thomas Dixon or Octavus Roy Cohen. When I asked Schuyler, in May 1975, whether he realized that "The Negro-Art Hokum" had been read as an "Uncle Tom" piece, he admitted wearily that he had frequently been misunderstood. In Schuyler's mind, to argue against a "peculiar" Negro art or psychology was not the same as denying the black heritage; indeed his main reason for writing "The Negro-Art Hokum," it seems, was to erase any feelings of racial inferiority on the part of Negro America. He was still attempting to "dispel the illusion of inferiority."

First, Schuyler argues in this essay that black art is not a racially unique expression (that is, there is no specific black aesthetic). Schuyler says:

True, from dark-skinned sources have come those slave songs based on Protestant hymns and Biblical texts known as the spirituals, work songs and secular songs of sorrow and tough luck known as the blues, that outgrowth of ragtime known as jazz (in the development of which whites have assisted), and the Charleston. . . . But these are contributions of a caste in a certain section of the country. They are foreign to Northern Negroes [Schuyler was a Northerner, of course], West Indian Negroes, and African Negroes. They are no more expressive or characteristic of the Negro race than the music and dancing of the Appalachian highlanders or the Dalmatian peasantry are expressive or characteristic of the Caucasian race. . . . It is merely a coincidence that this peasant class happens to be of a darker hue. . .[15]

Black literature "is identical in kind with the literature, painting, and sculpture of white Americans: that is, it shows more or less evidence of European influence."

Whether or not we might wish that Schuyler had at least attemp-

ted to develop a black aesthetic for the 1920s, we should realize that
thus far he was still very much in the mainstream of the 1920s. Black
literature, though perhaps devoted to black subjects, was stylisti-
cally true to American or European techniques (e.g., Imagism,
Realism, Naturalism, and the like). Black writers, such as Countee
Cullen or Claude McKay or Langston Hughes, wrote about the
African motherland or the horrors of lynchings, but usually in the
European or American style of the era.

So far Schuyler's essay was orthodox. But when he turned to a
discussion of the "differences" between black and white Americans,
he ruffled some feathers. Here's the most famous passage in the
essay:

. . . the Aframerican is merely a lampblacked Anglo-Saxon. If the European immigrant after two or three generations of exposure to our schools,
politics, advertising, moral crusades, and restaurants becomes indistinguishable from the mass of Americans of the older stock . . . , how much
truer must it be of the sons of Ham who have been subjected to what the
uplifters call Americanism for the last three hundred years. Aside from his
color, which ranges from very dark brown to pink, your American Negro is
just plain American. . . (662; my italics).

It is the impact of environment, caste, and culture—not color—that
distinguishes one people from another.

The phrase "lampblacked Anglo-Saxon" was unfortunate, but
Schuyler was intent on doing something other than "whitewashing"
black Americans. Quite simply, he was arguing against the prevalent notion that blacks are somehow different or "peculiar." The first
clue occurs in another passage:

Because a few writers . . . have seized upon imbecilities of the Negro
rustics and clowns and palmed them off as authentic and characteristic
Aframerican behavior, the common notion that the black American is so
"different" from his white neighbor has gained wide currency. The mere
mention of the word "Negro" conjures up in the average white American's
mind a composite stereotype of Bert Williams, Aunt Jemima, Uncle Tom,
Jack Johnson, Florian Slappey, and the various monstrosities scrawled by
the cartoonists. Your average Aframerican no more resembles this
stereotype than the average American resembles a composite of Andy
Gump, Jim Jeffries, and a cartoon by Rube Goldberg (662).

Later Schuyler returns to this theme. The "scribblings of Octavus

Cohen and Hugh Wiley," he writes, are not true reflections of
Negro Americans. That there is a distinctive Negro art, "is probably
the last stand of the old myth palmed off by Negrophobists for all
these many years, and recently rehashed by the sainted Harding,"
that there are "fundamental, eternal, and inescapable differences"
between white and black Americans (663). This myth:

has been broadcast all over the world by the vociferous scions of slave-
holders, "scientists" like Madison Grant and Lothrop Stoddard, and the
patriots who flood the treasury of the Ku Klux Klan; and is believed . . . by
the majority of free white citizens. On this baseless premise, so flattering to
the white mob, that the blackamoor is inferior and fundamentally different,
is erected the postulate that he must needs be peculiar; *and when he
attempts to portray life through the medium of art, it must of necessity be a
"peculiar" art* . . . (663; my italics).

It becomes apparent, then, that Schuyler's real purpose in the
essay was to discredit long-standing and entrenched stereotypes.
He wished to assert the humanity of black America, to prove once
and for all that Aframericans are not "fundamentally, eternally, and
inescapably different"—for to admit that (in Schuyler's view) was to
admit that "the blackamoor is inferior" and his art of necessity
"peculiar" (663).

After Hughes' article on "The Negro Artist and the Racial
Mountain" appeared, Schuyler tried again to clarify his position. In
a letter to the editor, Schuyler insisted that the black and white
masses are not all that different and that so-called "black art" is more
sectional than national. The artist, Schuyler reiterated, is the product of environment and education. And the great artist "is one who,
able to see life about him, and, struck by its quick interchange of
comedy, drama, and tragedy, attempts to portray it or interpret it in
music, poetry, or prose, on canvas or in stone. He can only use the
equipment furnished him by education and environment."[16] What
was clear to Schuyler was that propaganda (with its hint of special
pleading) was *not* the answer: "Negro propaganda-art, even while
glorifying the 'primitiveness' of the American Negro masses, is
*hardly more than a protest against a feeling of inferiority, and such
a psychology seldom produces art*" (my italics). Schuyler stuck to his
guns. In July 1926 he said:

why are most of us bellowing for NEGRO art, NEGRO literature, NEGRO

music, NEGRO dancing, etc! . . . Is it because we wish to be considered a
separate group, a different group? Are we not thus agreeing with Imperial
Wizard Evans and the late lamented Harding? If this is not true, why do we
continually emphasize color . . . ?[17]

But it is interesting to note that although Schuyler denounced the
emphasis on color, all of his fiction and essays were about the "color
problem" in the United States. When reading Schuyler, we rarely
doubt that he is a *black* writer. Schuyler did not write "raceless"
literature in the mode of, say, Frank Yerby. Schuyler just never did
practice what he preached in the 1920s. In 1930, Schuyler once
again stated his position, this time in response to a reader who asked
why "Amos 'n' Andy" was so popular with blacks as well as whites:

Amos 'n' Andy tickle the white folks for the reason that the spirituals tickle
them: i.e., they conform with the stereotype of the Negro manufactured by
white people for the purpose of justifying their treatment of the Negro.
Negroes enjoy both, along with the white oppressors, because . . . the
average Negro has the same attitude toward everything, including the
Negro, that the average Klansman has. The average Negro may not admit
this attitude but his actions and reactions speak louder than words. Day by
day . . . he disparages himself and his people, laughs at their misfortunes
and ignorance, lauds whiteness and decries blackness, shouts with glee at
the blackface comedians . . . and straightens his hair.
    Amos 'n' Andy, spiritual shouting, blackface comedians and all the
rest . . . help to bolster up the cannard of racial differences, the rock upon
which racial inequality is founded. *They salve the conscience of white
America for looting and robbing black America* by emphasizing that
Negroes are inferior, sentimental, sensual, ignorant, irresponsible children,
thus different from white folks and therefore not deserving of the same
treatment and consideration as other citizens (my italics).[18]

Schuyler could become furious when he felt that blacks had in
some way demeaned themselves in front of whites, as evidenced by
his reaction to an incident in 1930. Robert Russa Moton and a
commission of noted Afro-Americans were returning from Haiti by
ship. Apparently the white passengers asked the commission members to sing a few spirituals. They did. Schuyler ridiculed the
commission members as Uncle Toms and denounced spirituals as
"counterrevolutionary" and "defeatist." Then he made this militant
statement:

Negroes are engaged and have been for a long time in a bitter *war* for a place in this civilization as *full-fledged men and women.* That which *comforts and pleases the enemy cannot be beneficial.* . . . We are a great army moving forward to better things—a larger share of this world's goods and pleasures here and now, not when we die and go to roost on celestial bannisters. The true *soldier* thinks of victory on terra firma and not "pie in the sky, bye and bye" (my italics)[19].

The man who wrote "The Negro-Art Hokum" perhaps exaggerated, perhaps made statements that are no longer acceptable to black critics and writers. But it is hard indeed to conclude that he was an Uncle Tom. It was black Uncle Toms that Schuyler spent his life attacking.

CHAPTER 3

The Race Problem: Schuyler's Major Essays

W HILE much has been made of Schuyler's supposed assimilationism in "The Negro-Art Hokum," little has been said
about his race essays, which began appearing about the same time.
Yet they represent some of Schuyler's best analyses of the race
problem in the United States. They further reveal that Schuyler was
very much a 1920s race militant.

Of the dozens of articles Schuyler wrote on the race question, I
have selected seven that are considered his best efforts. "The Negro
and Nordic Civilization" (1925), "Blessed Are the Sons of Ham"
(1927), "Our White Folks" (1927), "Our Greatest Gift to America"
(1927), and "The Caucasian Problem" (1944) contain some of his best
satire. "A Negro Looks Ahead" (1930) and "Do Negroes Want to be
White?" (1956) are essentially nonsatiric. Two of the seven essays
appeared after the "literary years" and are discussed here because
they show Schuyler's progression from youthful idealism about a
"permanent solution" (interracial marriage) to despair over
America's inability to solve the race problem. Read in order, the
seven essays provide an important backdrop against which to consider *Black No More*.

I   Schuyler's Satiric Essays

"The Negro and Nordic Civilization" appeared in *The Messenger*
two years after Schuyler began his professional career. The essay
shows Schuyler attempting to develop a persona or narrator and a
tone of sustained irony. The persona begins by making what appears
to be a concession about the "superiority" of Nordic civilization:

I feel that we must admit in the face of a mountain of evidence that the

40

modern civilization of the Caucasian far excels anything developed by the Negro in Africa or elsewhere. . . . True, we have our gangsters, politicians, editorial writers and drug addicts, but these are largely due to an infusion of white blood . . . and the compelling force of environment.[1]

Perhaps with some luck Aframericans "may in another half century reach the Nordic level" (198); in the meantime they must "admit" their backwardness and earnestly endeavor to appreciate the benefits [they] are undoubtedly deriving from [their] association with the supermen" (199).

This rather heavy-handed irony evidences some race pride. In discussing black contributions to civilization, the persona makes another interesting "concession":

I am willing to concede . . . that the Negroes . . . contributed the foundations upon which Nordic civilization rests: the level, the wheel, the cam, the pulley, mathematics, paper, iron smelting, and, to go from the sublime to the ridiculous, much of what is known as Christianity. . . . I am even charitable enough to grant the Negroes such men as Antar, Pushkin, Dumas, . . . Toussaint L'Ouverture, Booker T. Washington and Henry O. Tanner. But who are such fellows . . . ? Surely we have never reached the level of Warren G. Harding! (201)

A somewhat more subtle piece, "Blessed Are the Sons of Ham," was Schuyler's second contribution to *The Nation* ("The Negro-Art Hokum" had appeared one year earlier). Again Schuyler employs a persona whose satiric premise is that whites "have looked upon the black citizen as a tragic figure . . . a helpless transplanted child of the jungle caught in the cruel meshes of machine civilization" (the "noble savage" theory in short) and hence "feel sorry" for the Negro who must daily face Jim Crow laws and racist slurs.[2] Actually, we are gravely informed, Negroes find white racism "continuously entertaining," (313). Entertaining? The narrator describes some of these "entertaining" incidents (drawn from Schuyler's own experiences) that "prove" how "blessed" the "sons of Ham" really are. For example, the narrator once tried to cash a check in a Paris, Texas, hotel. The white clerk insulted him in as many ways as possible, at first refused to cash his check and then wearily did so after the narrator made a "pest" of himself (314). That the clerk is forced to do anything for a "nigger" is so "amusing" that the narrator leaves the hotel laughing at the ways of white folks. The clerk's "discomfiture amused me" and gave "me a thrill and a laugh to help me on my journey" (314).

The response of the narrator, so reminiscent of Schuyler's own response during the Seattle bar incident (see Chapter 1), is partly the "laughing to keep from crying" response that blacks have had to develop. It is also Schuyler's way of thumbing his nose at white racists.

As long as the incidents in this essay are "amusing" (i.e., light enough so that the reader laughs with the narrator), "Blessed Are the Sons of Ham" is effective irony. Unfortunately, the still youthful Schuyler becomes carried away toward the end of his essay with indignation at white racism and provides examples that are not "amusing." He describes several incidents that evoke rage or fear instead of laughter (314-315). The inclusion of these incidents violates the unity of tone set at the beginning of the essay. In other words, the persona drops his ironic mask and lashes out directly at white racism.[3] It is a literary flaw that Schuyler learned to avoid in his mature pieces.

The lead article in the December 1927 *American Mercury,* "Our White Folks," was Schuyler's first piece for that famous publication. It was solicited by H.L. Mencken who, Schuyler told me in 1975, was not only *the* mentor of the era but a personal friend for many years.

In this essay, Schuyler employs a pattern he would use again and again: he first attacks white racists, then crosses over and attacks the black mentality which accepts the "White is Right" philosophy.[4] "To judge an individual solely on the basis of his skin color and hair texture is so obviously nonsensical that it seems not unreasonable to equate the bulk of Nordics with the *inmates of an insane asylum*" (my italics).[5] Indeed, "the Negro is a sort of black *Gulliver* chained by white *Lilliputians,* a prisoner in the jail of color prejudice" (385; my italics). After dissecting white prejudice, Schuyler focuses on blacks who have sold out by accepting the "White is Right" attitude. Specifically, he attacks skin whiteners and hair straighteners (as he does time and again in his columns, essays, and *Black No More*), while pointing to the proven abilities and rich history of black Americans. The Aframerican, he says, has had to be "more alert, more diplomatic, and a more skillful tactician than his white brothers" (387). He has always had a strong "pioneering spirit" as well as "energy and originality" (387). Indeed, the proud Aframerican can "put . . . the history of the blacks down through the ages alongside that of the whites and . . . not [be] ashamed":

He knows that there is as much evidence that black men founded human civilization as there is that white men did, and he doubts whether the occidental society of today is superior to the monarcho-communist society developed in Africa. . . . The average Negro is more alert, more resourceful, more intelligent, and hence more interesting than the average Nordic. Certainly if the best measure of intelligence is ability to survive in a changing or hostile environment, and if one considers that the Negro is not only surviving but improving all the time in health, wealth, and culture, one must agree that he possesses a high degree of intelligence (390).

This statement could hardly emanate from a man possessed by "the urge to whiteness." Neither could this graceful statement on the beauty of blackness:

Negroes possess within their group the most handsome people in the United States, with the greatest variety of color, hair and features. Here is the real melting pot, and a glorious sight to see. . . . The percentage of beautiful is unquestionably larger than among the ofay brethren (391).

Elsewhere the narrator amplifies: "Black? Well, yes, but how beautiful! How well it blends with almost every color! How smooth the skin; how soft and rounded the features. . . . Here in Aframerica one finds such an array of beauty that it even attracts Anglo-Saxons, despite their alleged color aversion" (392).

Published in *Ebony and Topaz* in 1927 and reprinted in V. F. Calverton's *Anthology of American Negro Literature* in 1929, "Our Greatest Gift to America" is probably Schuyler's most famous satiric essay. [6] The premise is deceptively simple—namely, that the "gift" is the mere *presence* of Negro Americans in the United States. Without blacks, the narrator informs us, white America would have no one to discriminate against. Further, blacks make the "gift" even more valuable by imitating whites (e.g., by trying to become as light as possible).

The narrator begins by poking fun at the Negro "intellectuals" who talk a lot but do nothing. He mocks "notable Aframerican speakers" in faddish Harlem Renaissance salons, men such as Professor Hambone of Moronia Institute and Dr. Lampblack of the Federal Society for the Exploitation of Lynching, who "eloquently hold forth for the better part of an hour on the blackamoor's gifts to the Great Republic" and completely miss the "greatest gift" (123). Such "Negro leaders" are accompanied by a New Negro poet who "recite[s] one of his inspiring verses anent a ragged black prostitute gnawing out her soul in the dismal shadows of Hog Maw Alley" (123). The irony is stinging, the references are clear: Professor

Hambone is almost certainly one of Schuyler's old enemies, Robert Russa Moton of Tuskegee; the young poet must be Claude McKay, author of the poem "Young Prostitute."

Proceeding to the average black American, the persona attacks those "smokes" who quite literally destroy their bodies (and souls) by trying to be white; they try to act "just like white folks" and scorn a fellow black man by saying that he acts "just like a nigger" (123).

Then Schuyler attacks the white mentality that feeds off the presence of an "inferior" people. One of his best portraits is of Dorothy Dunce, a "demure . . . packer in a spaghetti factory" whose "indulgent parents used to scare her by issuing a solemn warning that a big black nigger would kidnap her if she wasn't a good little girl" (123):

> She naturally believes . . . that every big, burly black nigger she meets on a dark street is ready to relieve her by force of what remains of her virtue. A value is placed upon her that she would not have in Roumania, Scotland, Denmark, or Montenegro. She is now a member of that exalted aggregation known as pure, white womanhood. She is also confident of her general superiority because education has taught her that Negroes are inferior, immoral, diseased, lazy, unprogressive, ugly, odiferous, and should be kept firmly in their place. . . . Quite naturally she swells with race pride, for no matter how low she falls, she will always be a white woman . . . (124).

Hence, "our presence . . . has been of incalculable value," for whites like Dorothy Dunce "have been buoyed up and greatly exalted by being constantly assured of their superiority. . ." (124). The Aframerican is America's "mudsill upon which all white people alike can stand and reach towards the stars" (124).

The irony in "Our Greatest Gift to America" is savage, specific, and well sustained. It is Schuyler at his best, and it moved Melvin Tolson, the respected black poet, to praise it as "the greatest satire on the race problem in this country that has ever been written. . . . It is Swift in one of his supreme moments."[7]

Significant as the articles already discussed are, it is only fair to Schuyler critics (and to Schuyler himself) to take notice of an optimistic piece called "A Negro Looks Ahead." In this essay, Schuyler unhesitatingly dismisses several current "solutions" to the race problem (return to Africa; physical separatism within the United States; separate economic development) and argues that the only logical solution is eventual "amalgamation with the Nordic population."[8] Indeed, someday current antimiscegenation laws will have been revoked, and blacks and whites will intermarry. By 2000 A.D. "a full-blooded American Negro may be rare enough to get a job in a museum"; a century hence "our American social leaders may be tanned naturally as they are now striving to become artificially" (219). In short, Schuyler bases his hopes on the melting pot theory.

Though such arguments may seem reasonable to some, for black American nationalists the article is an apparent sellout. Schuyler compounds the crime by insisting, as he had earlier in "The Negro-Art Hokum," that "the Aframerican is just a lampblacked Anglo-Saxon" (220).

Schuyler's theory of amalgamation, so idealistic in the 1920s, did not remain intact as racial problems in the United States grew worse during the 1930s and 1940s. Two essays that appeared after the 1923–1933 years show Schuyler moving toward a more despairing view of the situation. "The Caucasian Problem," published in Rayford Logan's *What the Negro Wants*, contains a hint of the despair to come. "Do Negroes Want to be White?", which appeared in *The American Mercury* in 1956, serves as a prophetic—and despairing—warning to the citizens of the United States.

II   *Schuyler's Non-Satiric Essays*

"The Caucasian Problem" is significant because, although Schuyler again urges racial amalgamation, his tone is considerably less sure than it had been in the past. "By a peculiar logical inversion," begins Schuyler, "the Anglo-Saxon ruling class, its imitators, accomplices and victims have come to believe in a Negro problem."[9] Such "propaganda" is "a great testimonial to the ingenuity of exploiters with a bad conscience; for while there is actually no Negro problem, there is definitely a Caucasian problem" (282). Ranging far both geographically and historically, Schuyler lays the blame at the feet of "the international capitalists who control the lives of over a billion colored people" (283); these capitalists are "practically all white," as are "the technicians, brokers, lawyers, generals, admirals, artists and writers who serve them" and have served them since the time of slavery, through colonialism, to the present. They have established "a vicious color caste system which makes [this] world a cultured hell" (284).[10]

Pointing out that terms like "Negro" and "Caucasian" are meaningless and that the myth of white superiority totally "ignores the findings of advanced sociologists and ethnologists," Schuyler continues:

the point is that these general terms . . . are convenient propaganda devices to emphasize the great gulf which we are taught to believe exists between these groups of people. It is significant that these divisions very conveniently follow the line of colonial subjugation and exploitation, with the Asiatics and Africans lumped together smugly as "backward peoples," "savages," "barbarians" or "primitives;" i.e., fair prey for fleecing and enslavement under the camouflage of "civilization" (287).

Warning that centuries of propaganda have to be undone, Schuyler argues with typical bluntness that "in the early days there was fraternization, intermixture and intermarriage between the masses of Negroes, whites and Indians in all the colonies;" had this been allowed to continue, he says, "there would now be no Caucasian problem" (288). What we need is to "re-condition colored and white people everywhere," to establish immediately "a revolutionary program of re-education calling not only for wholesale destruction of the accumulated mass of racialistic propaganda in books, magazines, newspapers, motion pictures and all the present [Jim Crow] laws . . . [but] a complete reorganization of our social system" (290):

It would have to include the complete abolition of Jim Crow laws and institutions; the rescinding of all racial pollution laws barring marriage because of so-called race; a complete enforcement of the letter and spirit of the federal constitution, and the ending of every vestige of the color bar in industry, commerce and the professions. The words "Negro," "white," "Caucasian," "Nordic" and "Aryan" would have to be permanently taken out of circulation . . . (293).

It is "extremely doubtful," Schuyler concludes, "that the colored people here or anywhere else will accept anything less than this" (296). The only alternative, he warns, "is to drift toward an international war" (297).

Schuyler tries to end his essay on a positive note, but he is well aware that "conflict and chaos" will probably polarize blacks and whites the world over:

there is still time to make a new world where tolerance, understanding, mutual respect and justice will prevail. . . . True, this means a complete about face on the part of the white world, but this is only right since the race problem is of its own making. The alternative here and abroad is conflict and chaos. We shall have to make a choice very soon (297-98).

Twelve years after the appearance of "The Caucasian Problem," Schuyler realized that "the choice" had still not been made. In "Do Negroes Want to be White?" he again describes various aspects of "this cultured hell," then notes that black Americans have no desire to be white: "The goal is not to be white but to be free in a white world," to gain "full and immediate citizenship rights under the Constitution."[11] White America is worried, he says, about "brownskin militancy and solidarity . . . a solidarity transcending petty divisions and appealing to pride of race" (57). Yet America is responsible for this militancy. Then Schuyler delivers the punchline in a passage that anticipates the Kerner Commission Report[12] by twelve years:

For better or for worse, two distinct, centripetal and endogamous societies have evolved in America. They seem to be as mutually exclusive as the Walloons and Flemings in Belgium. . . .
  Both now have a vested interest in their integrity. Few whites want to be black and few Negroes yearn to be white. There will always be a necessary measure of cooperation and liaison between them for the common good of all, but the idealists' vision [Schuyler's?] of an ultimate racial Melting Pot is, to say the least, dim and remote (58-9).

The young idealist of "A Negro Looks Ahead" has resigned himself to the reality of the American "insane asylum." America's absurd colorphobia has won out, the melting pot solution has become a "dim and remote" possibility. By 1956 the lonely iconoclast saw that America was "beyond cure." As we shall see in Chapter 5, Schuyler the satirist demonstrated this bitterness in *Black No More* twenty-six years before Schuyler the essayist admitted to despair in "Do Negroes Want to be White?"

CHAPTER 4

Black Art: Early Fiction and Sketches

I N the decade between 1923 and 1933, Schuyler wrote his major
sketches and short fiction. The first pieces were produced under
the pressure of deadlines for columns in *The Messenger;* they were
often short, propagandistic, and embarrassingly obvious.

By 1928, however, when "Woof" appeared in the single issue of
the magazine *Harlem,* Schuyler had matured as a writer. Thereafter
he wrote "Black Warriors," "Memoirs of a Pearl Diver," and "Black
Art," three skillfully developed sketches that revealed a more
mature journalist at work. By then his work was so good that Melvin
B. Tolson was moved to comment that "both as a writer and as a
man, George S. Schuyler is one of the most civilized personalities
that I have encountered on the American scene."[1]

In both his fiction and sketches, Schuyler remained loyal to his
basic subject matter—being black in America—and to his basic
theme—the insanity of black and white "colorphobia."

I Early Fiction

Young Schuyler, writing his "Aframerican Fables" in *The Messenger,* early turned to parodies such as "Coon River Anthology"
and "Fables" or to tall tales based on current events. The latter are
exemplified in a September 1926 "Fable" in which an Italian
bootlegger and his "high brown" girlfriend hit upon the ingenious
plan of importing "ofay females" into Harlem for black male clients.
The plan works well until black men become so race conscious that
they refuse to patronize "luscious" white women any more: "another
battle had been won for race consciousness [and] it was established
to the satisfaction of everyone that Nordic dames could no longer
lure the Ethiope from the charming maidens of his race"—a possibility, Schuyler snorts editorially, about as improbable as one of the
tall tales of Baron Munchhaussen. Such "fables" may demonstrate

Schuyler's race consciousness, but they include a minimum of good description and character development.[2]

"At the Coffeehouse," another early piece, is only somewhat better, containing the germ of an idea that would be developed more effectively by Wallace Thurman (*Infants of the Spring*, 1932) and by Langston Hughes (*The Ways of White Folk*, 1934). This piece satirizes white exploitation of the "New Negro vogue." In Schuyler's version, two white authors who are failing miserably in their profession determine to strike it rich by writing a "Negro story" stressing "shines in the stark Russian manner, . . . [the] African background with the throb of tom-toms, . . . racial memory, . . . [and] the thin veneer of white civilization crumbling off the educated darky and revealing the savage undercurrent"—in short, all those stereotyped images of the exotic-erotic primitive that Schuyler detested.[3] The two authors produce a wildly successful novel à la Carl Van Vechten which soon goes into a twenty-fifth printing! For scholars familiar with the "Harlem vogue" of the 1920s, "At the Coffeehouse" satirizes an all too familiar phenomenon.

"The Yellow Peril"[4] is a short play and a fairly effective piece of satire. An updated Harlem version of the "screen scene" in Sheridan's *School for Scandal*, it provides Schuyler with another opportunity to poke fun at the color bar in black society, especially the black man's obsession with light-skinned women. The same motif was used later by Wallace Thurman in *The Blacker the Berry* (1929).

Schuyler's play has one fairly well-developed character, the "high yaller" heroine, and several one dimensional types, her suitors, whom she must hide in various places in her apartment as new ones arrive to court "the yellow peril" with gifts. That there is little authorial intrusion suggests that Schuyler has matured to the point that he allows a story to tell itself. If the play has a major flaw, it is that the author is too concerned with the mechanics of the "screen scene." The dialogue, however, sparkles. One finishes the play agreeing wholeheartedly with the heroine's cynical observation: "It's easy to handle men because they're all saps. All you gotta do is to treat 'em as if they were ten years old" (31).[5] Interestingly enough, Charlie, the young hero who figures out and exposes the ruse, is the earliest version I have found of the Schuylerian *picaro*-trickster, a character who emerges fully defined in "Seldom Seen" and *Black No More*.[6]

Technically, "Seldom Seen"[7] is the best of Schuyler's early short stories. The young hero, Seldom Seen, is a handsome man of the world, the "sheik" of Baton Rouge, who "has the blues" because his proposals of marriage to Marie, an aristocratic though poverty-stricken near white Creole beauty, have been spurned. Marie, a genteel, virginal school teacher, refuses Seldom Seen because he is a gambler who "lives by his wits" and consorts with "citizens of the underworld"; Marie and her family "value . . . their social position, for they can boast of their descent from the French founders of Louisiana" (344).

Seldom Seen soon becomes involved with Bull Dog Clancy, the owner of a series of black barbershops and the most important bootlegger in the area. The two agree to help each other: Seldom Seen saves Clancy by purchasing and transporting for him a load of illegal whiskey for a local (white) Law and Order banquet; in exchange, Bulldog makes Seldom Seen a full partner in his "respectable" New Orleans Tonsorial Parlors. This gives the young hero the status Marie demands. When she learns that he has become respectable, "the little school teacher forgot her culture and social position" to become "eternal woman stalking her prey" (347). Seldom Seen allows himself to be "trapped," and the two are married. Marie, of course, never finds out about her lover's very lucrative underworld connections.

The story is effective for a variety of reasons. The love affair between hero and heroine develops logically and acceptably. The plot progresses along classical lines in terms of setting, conflict, action, and resolution. The characters are real, and the ironic tone is consistent.

Seldom Seen is a Schuylerian *picaro*-trickster, a lovable and handsome scoundrel who lives by his cunning, usually on the edge of the law, and who courts and finally wins the high class girl. The caste system and the color line are ridiculed (Seldom Seen, who marries a near white girl from a fine Louisiana family, anticipates Max in *Black No More*,[8] who marries a lily white girl from Atlanta) as a strong black man topples the rigid conventions of the South.

II *The American Mercury Sketches*

If "Seldom Seen" demonstrates Schuyler's maturing story-telling ability, his three *American Mercury* sketches in the early 1930s show his proficiency in the art of the character sketch. These pieces are gentle, often witty, anecdotal, and nostalgic portraits of people

Schuyler knew in the army ("Black Warriors"), during his Hobohemia days ("Memoirs of a Pearl Diver"), and as a child ("Black Art"). They reveal a black writer proud of his past, intrigued with black folklore, and always concerned with the real experiences of the ordinary man and woman. When asked if his sketches were true, Schuyler responded many years later that they were "almost entirely true."[9]

"Black Warriors," the first of the major pieces, was published in *The American Mercury* in 1930.[10] It is a series of six sketches of World War I "warriors" whom Schuyler knew in Hawaii. "Chicken-Breast," for example, had such a voracious appetite that he could be aroused out of a drunken stupor by a prankster playing the mess call. "Tush Morton" was an Irish brawler, the duty sergeant who outcursed, outdrank, outfought, and outsmarted his often mutinous. charges. "Pap Echols" was the over forty toughie who was finally whipped in a Honolulu brothel. "Broken Glasses" is the first version I have discovered of the Seattle bar incident (see Chapter 1), this time featuring the "company gambling king"— Rain-in-the-Face. "Sergeant Jackson" was the young black optimist who believed "the war would bring about a better understanding between the races"—until he was driven out of his hometown in Mississippi by a white mob. "The Company Banker," Hodge, was a graduate of Tuskegee, "full of the philosophy of the late and lamented Booker T. Washington" about "thrift, labor and innocence"—in wicked Honolulu. In each of these sketches the narrator stands well back from the action, allowing the characters to speak for themsleves as their brief tales unfold.

Schuyler's skill in character description is evident in his sketch of Pap Echols:

The recruiting officer must have been drunk when he enlisted Pap Echols. The old fellow was forty if he was a day. . . . He was short, brown and bowlegged and very closely resembled a gorilla. His head looked like an exaggerated nutmeg; his little red eyes were close together and popped out a surprising distance; his nose rambled over most of his face; his ears were elephantine and cauliflowered; his chin was rudimentary and his lips looked like frankfurters. . . . He was inured to vice, crime and liquor, and the constant threat of military prison did not cause him to mend his ways. . . (291).

Schuyler captures Pap's speech characteristics, especially his drunken bluster:

"Ah'm th' goddamdest, baddest niggah that evah come tuh this goddam
Army. Ah don't give uh damn 'bout nobody er nuthin'. Bettah not *nobody*
fool wi' me. Ah'll cutcha goddam hea't out an' stuff it down yo goddam
th'oat. . ." (291–92).

When Pap is called a liar during a crap game by a monster named
"Bear," Pap proves his in-fighting abilities: "The old fellow's eyes
narrowed, and, rising quickly, he seized the box on which he had
been seated and brought it down on Bear's head. Then, as his
tormentor lay helpless . . . he kicked him in the face with his No. 12
shoes for good measure. It all happened with lightning swiftness"
(292).

   "Memoirs of a Pearl Diver" appeared in *The American Mercury*
the following year.[11] Again Schuyler employed his already successful pattern of describing men and incidents in an environment he
knew, in this case the various greasy spoon restaurants he worked in
during the early 1920s. At Weinstine's, for example, the over-
worked and not yet paid workers hatch a beautiful scheme for a sit
down strike in order to get better working conditions and back pay.
The result is a collective *picaro* action that anticipates *Black No
More*. Anoter sketch involves the men who work at the Alford
Lunch, an international crew including a German, a Pole, a Russian,
a West Indian, a British cockney, an Irishman, two Columbians—a
"low-life" League of Nations. As there is constant warfare among the
various nationalities, the proprietor has to maintain a precarious
peace by siding with each offended and/or enraged crewman:

When fights arose between members of the crew, Sam Karlin, the boss,
took the role of peacemaker. He very shrewdly sympathized with all points
of view. To the Irish he denounced England; he sided either with the
Russian or the Pole, depending on which he was talking to; he was
Republican, Democrat or Socialist as circumstance demanded; within the
period of five minutes he would tell George that Marcus Garvey was greater
than Napoleon and assure Clarence that the Provisional President of Africa
was a damn fool (494).

Another sketch concerns Mrs. Williams, a little old gentlelady
whose immaculate dining room becomes a "concession stand" for a
"gang of pirates . . . bums . . . wastrels," members of a brawling
construction crew with whom Schuyler worked. Because Mrs.
Williams insists on sitting at the head of the table at each meal, all
profanity, sloppy eating, and grubby dressing miraculously disap-

pear. So do the men's appetities, especially when they have to
participate in before meal prayers. The foreman, aware that his men
are not eating (and therefore not working) right, apprehensively asks
Mrs. Williams to let his crew eat alone. After she graciously agrees
to remove herself at mealtime, the men return to their normal
habits, one of them noting that "Now a guy kin feel at home aroun'
dese diggin's" (496). A typical Damon Runyon tale, this sketch has a
surprising yet realistic ending.

Without doubt, "Black Art" is the best of Schuyler's sketches.[12]
In it he creates in loving detail a lifelike portrait of his grandmother,
who is not only a study in black art herself but a woman who has had
extensive experience with the "black art" of witchcraft. The sketch
also features a small boy, Schuyler himself, and his wide-eyed
fascination with and abortive experiments in witchcraft. The piece
incorporates a considerable amount of Northern black folklore,
allowing Schuyler to record Yankee myth in much the same manner
that Zora Neale Hurston (a woman Schuyler greatly admired[13])
recorded Southern myth:

The grandmother [we learn] was walnut colored and of great girth, with
wavy gray-streaked black hair severely parted in the middle and balled up
over the ears, a determined mouth, and dark penetrating eyes. Sitting in
her rocker by the reading table, with her silver-rimmed spectacles perched
precariously on the top of her nose and the light from the kerosene lamp's
flowered globe softening the fine little wrinkles on her face, she resembled
an old Dutch painting (335).

The grandmother over a period of time relates a series of six
(interlocking) tales of witches and demons. She tells of "the conjurer
who could twist off his head and walk around with it talking loudly
on the palm of his hand" (337); the colonial mansion which before
the Revolution was the scene of a beautiful ball during which all the
dancers were murdered by Indians—and which by Schuyler's time
had become on certain nights "mysteriously illuminated . . . while
graceful, bewigged couples passed back and forth before the win-
dows" (338); "Black Tom" the powerful conjurer who "carried a
hook-handed cane, the tapping of which could be heard a great
distance":

When he grew thirsty and did not find the tavern liquor to his liking, he
would hang a sizeable jug on the handle of his cane and send it off stumping
by itself into the deep woods while he sat amidst profound silence and

smoked. Shortly the cane would return with the jug overflowing with excellent corn liquor (338).

She tells of an old African slave who put a curse upon an entire family of slaves until he was freed and who then became the "right-hand man of Satan." He played the fiddle at barn dances but, like the characters in numerous fairy tales, the dancers had to beware: "woe be to those thoughtless dancers who failed to quit before the fateful hour of midnight, for then this fiddler became possessed of the Devil, and played the weirdest tunes . . . which compelled the dancers to jig all day Sunday or until they fell. . . ." (338–39). Grandma also told of the "stooped old black woman, Mrs. Croman," who told fortunes and "was on more than speaking acquaintance with the Devil" (340).

Hearing these many tales, young Schuyler determines to try "his own hand at the black art." He decides to master the violin, "even though he must enter the service of Satan" if he wishes to become a great artist (still another meaning of the term "black art"). Schuyler describes his midnight "initiation" in terms reminiscent of Washington Irving's "The Legend of Sleepy Hollow" or Mark Twain's *Tom Sawyer* (Schuyler told me he admired both authors):

I decided to go on and sell my soul and become a great violinist, filling opera houses with enthusiastic audiences. . . .
Sneaking out of the house at eleven o'clock, I hurried across the moonlit fields to my rendezvous with Satan. I sat down on a big boulder to play. The evening seemed almost chilly for summer, and I never imagined that there were so many noises in the . . . silence of the night. Leaves rustled, twigs broke, frogs croaked. My ambition to become a great violinist waned with the increasing strain on my nerves; when, steeling myself, I drew the first mournful discord on the fiddle, it [my ambition] disappeared altogether. In an astonishing short time I found myself back home, alternately panting and shivering. . . .
Next day, when I shamefacedly recounted my adventures to Grandma, the old lady cackled until tears rolled down her wrinkled cheeks and her belly shook as if moved by inner springs. She wiped her eyes . . . and said in a soft and tender way, "You damned little fool!" (342).

Striking just the proper balance between the wide-eyed curiosity of a young child and the gentle cynicism of that same child grown up, Schuyler deftly imbues his characters, his plot, and his tone with a nostalgia that makes "Black Art" a most delightful piece. It led Melvin B. Tolson to write a letter describing his friendship with and admiration for Schuyler:

Once I heard Mrs. Schuyler say that the ironist had a streak of sentiment in him. . . . I had not been able to discover that trait in his writings until I read "Black Art." . . . Grandma is an unforgettable character. She is delineated with sympathetic understanding against a perfect background. The sketch is rich in its revelations. It is *truly interpretative of Negro lowly life*. It has the golden ring (my italics).[14]

As we approach *Black No More*, it is worthwhile noting that Tolson also had words of praise for Schuyler the satirist: "He stimulates more differences of opinion than any other Negro writer," (374) Tolson said. Schuyler's views are "attacked and defended" in barber shops, railroad cars, "pool rooms, classrooms, churches, and drawing rooms" (374). Schuyler's critics, Tolson said, "usually miss the point" and "run from the sublime to the ridiculous" (374). Tolson, incidentally, not only devoted a chapter of his Master of Arts thesis on "The Negro or Harlem Renaissance" to Schuyler in 1940, but he adapted and dramatized *Black No More* in 1952.[15]

CHAPTER 5

Black No More *Revisited*

T HE first full-length satire by a black American writer and *the* satire of the Harlem Renaissance, *Black No More* was assuredly Schuyler's greatest literary effort. W. E. B. Du Bois, though himself lampooned in the book, received it enthusiastically: "It is a satire, a rollicking, keen, good-natured criticism of the Negro problem in the United States, following the same method by which Bernard Shaw has been enabled to criticize the social organizations of the modern world."[1]

Sometime during 1930, according to Schuyler, V. F. Calverton "encouraged me to write my first book, . . . a satire on the American race question, which was the first, I believe, to treat the subject with levity."[2] He told me in May 1975 that he worked on the book "about six or seven months," and then sent it to Macaulay, the publishing house, where it was well received. Macaulay issued *Black No More* in January 1931.

I *The Plot of* Black No More: *Probable Absurdities*

Schuyler's plot runs true to a fundamental satiric premise— namely, that no matter how fantastic the premise, the plot "pretends to be true and real."[3] Further, like the satires of Schuyler's models, including Horace, Juvenal, Swift, and Twain, *Black No More* is topical (race relations in the United States), pretends to present a real picture of the way people behave, and is built on the assumption that the human condition is primarily ridiculous. If the plot seems exaggerated or distorted, it is only because the reader is too dull or naive to realize the true state of the world.

Schuyler used the usual satiric devices to build his novel. One such device is *reductio ad absurdum* or reduction to absurdity, whereby he takes existing conditions and extends them only slightly until we see the fundamental absurdity of man's behavior. Another device he employs is projection, whereby he leads the reader from the definite present into the possible future (the action occurs between 1933 and 1940). Still another traditional plot device Schuyler employs is the picaresque narrative, which allows for an episodic, loosely structured plot in which the action ranges far and wide.

If we consider the Preface an integral part of the novel, *Black No More* has three fairly distinct divisions: in Part I, we encounter prevailing reality; in Part II, we move from reality into absurdity as well as meeting the *picaro* protagonist; and in Part III we see the logical results of that absurdity.

In the Preface, the narrator informs us that *Black No More* is subtitled "an account of the strange and wonderful workings of science in the land of the free, A.D. 1933–1940" and is dedicated to "all Caucasians in the great republic who can trace their ancestry back ten generations and confidently assert that there are no Black leaves, twigs, limbs, or branches on their family trees."[4] The narrator then identifies his major enemies—white racists, black leaders who betray their people, and the cosmeticians who capitalize on America's "colorphobia." Many chemists, the narrator says (truthfully enough) "have been seeking the means for making the downtrodden Aframerican resemble as closely as possible his white fellow citizens" (7). Chemical preparations currently on the market "have so far proved exceedingly profitable to manufacturers, advertising agencies, Negro newspapers and beauty culturists. . . ." (7). "Millions of [black] users," he continues, "have registered great satisfaction at the opportunity to rid themselves of kinky hair and grow several shades lighter in color" (7).[5] Always present is "America's constant reiteration of the superiority of whiteness" (7).

Science, he continues, has made a few breakthroughs in its "avid search . . . for some key to chromatic perfection" (7). For example, one Dr. Yusaburo Noguchi revealed in October 1929 that he could "change a Negro into a white man by using a treatment involving glandular control and electrical nutrition" (7–8). Absurd? Not so. In *The Pittsburgh Courier*,[6] a front page article about a Dr. Yusaburo Noguchi was headlined: "Racial Metamorphosis Claimed By Scientist: Japanese Says He Can Change Black Skin Into White. . . ." The article claims that Noguchi's treatments "include the use of sun rays, ultra-violet rays, special diets and glandular treatments." Claiming that "racial characteristics . . . are the result of a combination of glandular secretions and physical environment," the Japanese scientist is quoted as saying that "racial metamorphosis could not be effected overnight" but that, given time, he "could change the Japanese into a race of tall, blue-eyed blonds." That Schuyler remembered this article nearly a year later is obvious; he directly quotes its final line in his Preface!

58 GEORGE S. SCHUYLER

Part II begins with the first chapter, in which we meet Max Disher, the protagonist, in a typical Harlem sequence. A Harlem dandy, Max discusses with his friend Bunny various "women of color," debating the glories of the "high yaller" (one of whom had just snubbed Max) as opposed to the "plug ugly" black woman (18–20). The discussion is a painful parody of a dominant attitude of the 1920s, that white women are the most beautiful, "high yallers" the next most beautiful, and so forth, down through browns to "coal" blacks.[7]

The second sequence is a deft parody of the familiar Harlem nightclub scene.[8] Max and Bunny enter the Honky-Tonk Club where "blacks, browns, yellows, and whites [were] chatting, flirting, drinking; rubbing shoulders in the democracy of night life" (20). A floorshow features "a black-faced comedian, a corpulent shouter of mammy songs with a gin-roughened voice, three chocolate softshoe dancers and an octette of wriggling, practically nude, mulatto chorines" (22). Soon a party of downtown whites sweeps in, and Max falls in love with a "tall, slim, titian-haired girl" (Helen) who "seemingly stepped from Heaven or the front cover of a magazine" (20). Max asks her to dance with him in this "democracy of night life"; her reply (in a Southern drawl) introduces a note of jarring realism in the otherwise romantic scene: "No . . . I never dance with niggers!" (23).

Helen's refusal so irritates Max that he decides he must win her. The next day he learns that an old friend, Dr. Junius Crookman, has returned from Germany; the black doctor has discovered a process whereby he can change black skin to white and make kinky hair straight. Max decides to undergo the ultimate "process" and pass over into the white world.[9]

Crookman and his two black underworld associates, Hank Johnson and Chuck Foster, quickly organize Black-No-More, Inc., a series of sanitariums across the country where Negroes are whitened in three days for fifty dollars. Max just barely beats the Harlem mob to the door and is the first to sign up.

The scene in which Max is whitened is a good example of the death and rebirth motif that Ralph Ellison later employed effectively in *Invisible Man:*

He [Max] quailed as he saw the formidable apparatus of sparkling nickel. It resembled a cross between a dentist's chair and an *electric chair*. Wires and straps, bars and levers protruded from it and a great nickel headpiece . . . hung over it. . . . He gasped with fright and would have made for the door but the two husky attendants held him firmly, stripped off his robe and *bound him in the chair.* There was no retreat. *It was either the beginning or the end* (my italics).[10]

Max Disher is reborn as Matthew Fisher and emerges from the Black-No-More sanitarium: "he felt terribly weak, emptied and nauseated; his skin twitched and was dry and feverish; his insides felt very hot and sore" (34). He soon realizes, however, that "he [is] free"—free of the "kink-no-more-lotions" and the weekly "expenditures for skin whiteners" (35). He now has the "open sesame of a pork-colored skin!" (35).

The third and longest part of the book traces the effects of Black-No-More on American society. It includes the adventures of Max and Bunny in the South, the reaction of black race leaders to the threat of Black-No-More (it puts them out of the "leadership" business), and the frantic reaction of white America, especially in the South. All three narrative threads are held together by the adventures of Max and Bunny.

As soon as Max passes over, he proceeds to Atlanta in search of Helen. As he also needs a job, he decides the best "con" in the South is the Black-No-More "menace" itself, so he infiltrates the Knights of Nordica, recently revived by Reverend Henry Givens, posing as an anthropologist and race expert. His inflammatory lectures on the "menace" impress the knights and they make him their Grand Exalted Giraw. He also finds and marries Helen, who turns out to be Givens' daughter. After he lines his pockets with money from the Knights of Nordica coffers, Max, with Bunny, exploits first the increasingly violent labor situation and then Southern politics. By 1936, the two *picaros* have managed to propel Henry Givens and Arthur Snobbcraft, head of the lily white Anglo-Saxon Association, into national prominence as the Democratic presidential and vice-presidential candidates who will forge a new dixiecrat coalition. Max is not exposed until the end of the book, when Helen gives birth to a mulatto child; Max, Helen, Bunny, and the baby barely escape enraged Southern mobs and fly to Europe with the money they have extorted.

Max's adventures occur against an increasingly ugly white American backdrop. First, America loses its cheap "nigger" labor, so it must hire poor whites (many of whom are really ex-blacks) who promptly strike for higher wages and better working conditions. Second, when white parents learn that their daughters will produce

mulatto children if they marry ex-Negroes, they revive the old
"would you want your daughter to marry. . . ." question. Crookman
and his associates quickly set up lying-in hospitals in which babies
are "processed" in twenty-four hours.

Inevitably, the "menace" becomes the central issue of the 1936
national elections. As the campaign heats up, Givens and Snobbcraft
(unknown to Max) establish a supersecret research project, headed
by Samuel Buggerie, the purpose of which is to separate true
whites from whitened Negroes and to "get a genealogical law
passed disfranchising all people of Negro or unknown ancestry"
(154). To protect its investment, meanwhile, Black-No-More,
Inc., contributes five million dollars to insure the reelection of
President Goosie.

The story rapidly climaxes. The secret research project backfires
when Buggerie learns that over half the white American population
has "tainted" blood, including the leaders of the Ango-Saxon Association, the Knights of Nordica, and the supposedly lily white
families of the South. Before he can suppress his inflammatory
report, Buggerie is robbed by the Republican Party (specifically by
three or four ex-blacks), and his report is published in the newspapers. America goes berserk. Mobs search out the new "niggers,"
now the leaders of the Democratic Party. Senator Kretin,
Snobbcraft, Buggerie, and others are lynched, riots occur throughout the South—and the Republicans are returned to office.

As a reward for services (and monies) rendered, President Goosie
makes Dr. Crookman the U.S. surgeon-general. Later, in 1940,
Crookman reveals to the nation that all whitened Negroes in
America are really "two or three shades *lighter* than the old Caucasians" (218; my italics). America is thrown into a frenzy when it
learns that white is *not* right. Panicked citizens purchase skin-
darkening lotions (Egyptienne Stain; Zulu Tan), sunbathing becomes a national hobby, light-skinned whites are discriminated
against, and America becomes—in the final absurdity—"definitely,
enthusiastically mulatto-minded" (22). In short, by the end of the
novel, things return to "normal"—except that now black is beautiful!

II *Characterization: Of Villains and Black Picaros*

One aspect of Schuyler's satire that is immediately recognizable
is his giving of obvious descriptive names to his characters, much in

the manner of Sheridan or Dickens. Thus, Dr. Crookman is the "crook" who cons the entire American population with his final "solution" to the race problem; Mme. Blandish is the Harlem "beauty queen" who specializes in lightening black skins; Senator Kretin is a Southern politician whose intelligence quotient is incredibly low; Snobbcraft is the snootily aristocratic leader of the Anglo-Saxon Association; Dr. Buggerie is a researcher whose gender is not pure; Bunny Brown, Max's cherubic accomplice, resembles Brer Rabbit; the Reverend McPhule (rhymes with "fuel") delights in burning "niggers"; the Knights of Nordica are white supremacists; Professor Handen Moutthe is an inept researcher; the Right Reverend Bishop Ezekiel Whooper heads the Ethiopian True Faith Wash Foot Methodist Church; and Forkrise Sake is a Japanese-American country and western musician of dubious talents.

But Schuyler does more than give his characters obvious names. While the plot of satire may pretend to be real, the characters "although often described with every appearance of gravity, are misshapen, exaggerated, and caricatured."[11] Schuyler is a master of caricature, of lampooning existing individuals by selecting characteristics of that person and exaggerating them to the point of absurdity. He is also a master of parody, a satiric device whereby a person's speaking or writing style is exaggerated for comic effect. Schuyler demonstrates his skill in these two areas when he takes an existing person, such as W. E. B. Du Bois, and turns him into Dr. Shakespeare Agamemnon Beard.

Dr. Beard is a crafty, scheming black leader who calls together the other black leaders in America, except Santop Licorice (Marcus Garvey),[12] to determine some action against Black-No-More, Inc. He is the principal spokesman for the National Social Equality League (the NAACP) and the editor of *The Dilemma (The Crisis)*. He is "a graduate of Harvard, Yale and Copenhagen" (Du Bois attended Harvard and the University of Berlin) and is noted for his "haughty bearing" which "never failed to impress both Caucasians and Negroes" (scholars have remarked that Du Bois was "patrician and chilly"). He has a "curly gray head . . . and full spade beard" (90; Du Bois had a Vandyke beard). The caricature continues:

For a mere six thousand dollars a year [Dr. Beard] . . . wrote scholarly and biting editorials in *The Dilemma* denouncing the Caucasians whom he secretly admired and lauding the greatness of the Negroes whom he alternately pitied and despised. In limpid prose he told of the sufferings and privations of the downtrodden black workers with whose lives he was thankfully unfamiliar. Like most Negro leaders, he deified the black woman but abstained from employing aught save octoroons. He talked at white banquets about "we of the black race" and admitted in books that he was part-French, part-Russian, part-Indian, and part-Negro. He bitterly denounced the Nordics for debauching Negro women while taking care to hire comely yellow stenographers with weak resistance (90).

Some of the references are recognizable. Du Bois was a scholar, a warrior (Agamemnon) for equal rights and a creative writer (Shakespeare). He co-founded the NAACP, edited *The Crisis* (for which he wrote many editorials), organized four Pan-Africa conferences, lectured, and produced a number of seminal works such as *The Souls of Black Folk* on black history and sociology.

Yet at the same time the portrait is highly exaggerated for comic effect. Dr. Beard emerges as a stock hypocrite, a sin that many a satirist has excoriated. He earns "a mere six thousand dollars a year" (a princely sum in the 1920s); he "secretly admires" Caucasians though he attacks them publicly; he "pitied and despised" the black masses (perhaps a reference to Du Bois' early middle class orientation or his theory of the "talented tenth"); he claims "exotic" instead of "common" blood (Du Bois did claim French Huguenot ancestry), thus further setting himself apart from the people he supposedly serves; he lusts after "high yallers" and octoroons instead of the black women he publicly champions (Du Bois did praise black women in pieces like "The Black Mother"[13]). In short, Schuyler creates an exaggerated picture of an existing person. At the same time, his creation becomes a universally recognizable "leader of the people" who makes a fortune off human misery, a greedy man willing to curry favor with the majority, an elitist and, above all, a hypocrite.

When Schuyler parodies Du Bois' speaking and writing style, he mimics his more flowery style. Thus, Dr. Beard addresses the assembled race leaders in this manner:

It were quite unseemly for me who lives such a cloistered life and am spared the bane or benefit of many intimate contacts with those of our struggling race who by sheer courage, tenacity and merit have lifted their heads above the mired mass, to deign to take from a more capable individual the unpleasant task of reviewing the combination of circumstances that has brought us together, man to man, within the four walls of the office (92–93).

All this in one sentence? Here Schuyler mocks the turgid prose Du Bois was capable of in, say, "Of the Passing of the First Born" in *The Souls of Black Folk*. In another speech, Dr. Beard rhapsodizes on Africa in the manner of a mediocre eighteenth century epic poet:

our destiny lies in the stars. Ethiopia's fate is in the balance. The goddess of the Nile weeps bitter tears at the feet of the Great Sphinx. The lowering clouds gather over the Congo and the lightning flashes o'er Togoland. To your tents, O Israel! The hour is at hand (92).[14]

Incredibly, all of Africa has responded emotionally to the perils Black-No-More, Inc., represents. We are so swept away by the passion that we almost miss the idiocy. One short passage includes an address to a goddess, epic—if somewhat mangled—scope, archaic language ("lowering," "o'er"), pathetic fallacy, and hyperbole.[15]

Had Schuyler only attacked black leaders, we might question his loyalties. But he also attacks other, more insidious race "leaders," such as those who profited in the cosmetics industry. Mme. Sisseretta Blandish owns the "swellest hair-straightening parlor in Harlem" (47). She specializes in straightening hair and lightening skin, yet, hypocritically, she denounces Max after he "crosses over": "I always said niggers didn't really have any race pride" (47).

Mme. Blandish is a "fat brown woman" who wears "voluminous dresses" that "drape her Amazonian form" (47–48; 59): "Because of her prominence as the proprietor of a successful enterprise engaged in making Negroes appear as much like white folks as possible, she had recently been elected for the fourth time a Vice-President of the American Race Pride League" (59). But her hair-straightening and skin-whitening business becomes irrelevant with the rise of Black-No-More, Inc., so Mme. Blandish "passes over" and becomes Mrs. Sari Blandine (221). At the end of the novel, when "whites" are desperately seeking to become darker, the ever-resourceful "beauty queen" makes a comeback by developing a "skin-stain that . . . imparted a long-wearing light-brown tinge to the pigment" (221) and by patenting "Blandine's Egyptienne Stain" (221).

In this character, Schuyler appears to be caricaturing two people, Mme. C. J. Walker and her daughter, L'Alelia. Mme. Walker went to St. Louis in 1905, "hit on a formula for *improving the appearance* of the hair of the Negro" (my italics), developed a mail-order business, and by 1910, established "laboratories for the manufacture of various cosmetics."[16] She died in 1919. Her daughter inherited the

estate. In that same year, the International League of Darker
People (probably Schuyler's "American Race Pride League") was
formed at the Walker estate in New York. L'Alelia, a social lioness
during the Harlem Renaissance, was in physique much like
Schuyler's caricature. According to Langston Hughes, L'Alelia was
the "big-hearted, night-dark, hair-straightening heiress," a "gor-
geous Amazon, in a silver turban. . . ."[17]
    If anything, Schuyler's ridicule of white villains is even more
devastating. As Du Bois noted in 1931, *Black No More* not only
contains "scathing criticism of Negro leaders" but "passes over and
slaps the white people just as hard and unflinchingly straight in the
face."[18]
    Schuyler's white villains are legion. Many of them are generic
types, such as the corrupt politician, the lily white Southern aristocrat, the big businessman, the KKKer, and the fundamentalist
preacher.[19] Some of these types appear as Gorman Gay, chairman of
the Republican National Committee; Mr. Gump, vice-president of
the United States; the Honorable Walter Brybe, "who had won his
exalted position as Attorney General of the United States because of
his long and faithful service helping large corporations to circum-
vent the federal laws" (99); Mortimer K. Shanker, an announcer for
station WHAT in Atlanta; the Reverend John Whiffle and Bishop
Belch, both of whom are more interested in politics than religion;
Senator Kretin, a white Southern politician; Dr. Samuel Buggerie, a
lily white Virginia aristocrat and researcher of the inane; and the
Reverend Alex McPhule, the quintessential fanatical preacher.
    Other white characters are caricatures of specific people. Presi-
dent Harold Goosie is probably Herbert Hoover. The Reverend
Henry Givens is probably a composite of two 1920s Klan
leaders—William Joseph Simmons and Edward Clark Young. Arthur Snobbcraft, the president of the Anglo-Saxon Association, is
John Powell of the Anglo-Saxon Clubs in Virginia; and Senator
Kretin may well be Senator Blease of South Carolina. The characters of Givens and Snobbcraft deserve more attention.
    Schuyler's archetypal Southern racist, the Reverend Henry Giv-
ens, is a "short, wizened, almost-bald, bull-voiced, ignorant ex-
evangelist" who revitalized the Klan after World War I (67) and
made a fortune off ignorant Southern whites eager to receive his
"message" (68): "Not only had [he] . . . toiled diligently to increase
the prestige, power, and membership of the defunct Ku Klux Klan,
but he had also been a very hard worker in withdrawing as much

money from its treasury as possible" (67–68). Greed and the threat
of Black-No-More, Inc., tempt Givens to resurrect a Klan type
organization.
   Givens' greed is matched only by his stupidity. When Max
appears at his headquarters to offer his services as an "anthropologist," Givens gladly accepts his help—though he has no
idea of what an anthropologist is. When Max departs, Givens

reached over, and pulled the dictionary stand toward him and opened the
big book to A.
   "Lemme see, now . . . Anthropology. Better git that word straight 'fore I
go talkin' too much about it". . . . He read over the definition . . . twice
without understanding it. . . (71).

Givens' career develops rapidly once the newly whitened Max
becomes his amanuensis. Combining anti-Communism, religious
fanaticism, and hate, Givens exhorts the knights about the sociological, religious, scientific, and cultural dangers of Black-No-More.
Givens, "who had finished the eighth grade in a one-room country
school, explained the laws of heredity and spoke eloquently of the
growing danger of black babies" (110).
   On his way to acquiring the 1936 presidential nomination, Givens
(the wily Max preparing the way) schedules a spectacular, nation-
wide radio program to broadcast the dangers of Black-No-More. The
program is replete with a black-faced minstrel singing "Vanishing
Mammy" (Al Jolson?), a supersquare radio announcer, and a country
and western band. Givens speaks on "The Menace of Negro Blood."
Fortified with whiskey, he talks for an hour, "successfully avoiding
saying anything that was true" (149); he discusses "the foundations
of the Republic, anthropology, miscegenation, co-operation with
Christ, getting right with God, curbing Bolshevism, the bane of
birth control, the menace of the Modernists, science versus religion, and many other subjects of which he was totally ignorant" (149).
Native cunning, good public relations, and a genius for alliteration
catapult Givens into the national limelight. Only when the
genealogical study to trace tainted blood backfires must Givens give
up his dream of the presidency and admit that "we're all niggers
now" (193).
   Givens may well be a caricature of an itinerant Methodist
preacher named William Joseph Simmons,[20] who revived the Klan
in 1915 in Atlanta. A "colonel" in the Woodmen of the World, he

liked fraternal organizations. He was, apparently, "an effective speaker, with an affinity for alliteration" and preached on topics such as "Women, Wedding, and Wives" or the "Kinship of Kourting and Kissing." As Imperial Wizard of the Invisible Empire of the Knights of the Ku Klux Klan, he built up an effective membership and a treasury with the help of Edward Clark Young and Elizabeth Tyler, two press agents and fund raisers par excellence. Membership in the Klan topped four million in its heyday in the mid-1920s; the KKK was powerful enough to affect both the 1924 and the 1928 presidential campaigns.

Simmons, Young, and Tyler developed a systematic philosophy of hate. The Klan's enemies were "booze, loose women, Jews, Negroes, Roman Catholics (whose 'dago Pope' was bent on taking over the U.S.), and anybody else who was not a native-born white Protestant Anglo-Saxon." Methodist and Baptist clergymen "lent the KKK massive support."[21]

If Givens is the compleat Klansman, Arthur Snobbcraft, president of the Anglo-Saxon Association, is a perfect caricature of the old Virginia aristocrat. He is one of the "rich highbrows who can trace [his] ancestry back almost two hundred years" (152) and is therefore one of those Schuyler had in mind when he dedicated his book to whites who "trace their ancestry back ten generations" to prove "that there are no Black leaves, twigs, limbs or branches on their family trees."

Snobbcraft is "the genius that thought up the numerous racial integrity laws adopted in Virginia and many of the other Southern states" (154). He is "strong for sterilization of the unfit, meaning Negroes, aliens, Jews and other riff raff, and he had an abiding hatred of democracy" (154). Though he despises the Knights of Nordica (it "contained just the sort of people he wanted to legislate into impotency"), he is willing to form an alliance in order to create a power bloc to destroy Black-No-More, Inc. He even succeeds (again with Max's help) in acquiring the vice-presidential nomination. Wealthy, disdainful, aristocratic, Snobbcraft too has his weakness—he craves political power: "These men [Snobbcraft and the Virginia elite] had dreamed from youth of holding high political office at the national capital. . . . By swallowing their pride . . . and joining with the riff raff of the Knights . . . they saw an opportunity . . . to get into power; and they took it" (155). Snobbcraft and Buggerie take it upon themselves to separate lily white from "tainted" Americans. To his horror, Snobbcraft learns that his ancestors were "in what you call the lower orders: . . . laboring people, convicts, prostitutes, and that sort. One of your maternal ancestors in the late seventeenth century was the off-spring of an English serving maid and a black slave" (179). Snobbcraft must accept the bitter truth that "over half the population has no record of its ancestry beyond five generations" (177).

Snobbcraft, although a type, is probably a caricature of a person with whom James Weldon Johnson crossed swords in 1924.[22] John Powell of Virginia wrote an article in *The New York World* (December 2, 1924) in which he explained the philosophy of the various Anglo-Saxon Clubs in the South. In brief, Mr. Powell deplored the "polyglot boarding house" aspect of America and announced that Anglo-Saxon purity and culture were menaced by Negroes and other "aliens." He assured his readers that only Anglo-Saxons were fit for leadership. Quickly—and scathingly for him—Johnson rebutted Powell in an article which appeared in *The World* (February 3, 1924). But the "discussion" was never conclusively laid to rest. Such material is still disseminated.[23]

In contrast to the various white and black villains is the protagonist—Max—a black *picaro* in whose character Schuyler merged both European and black folklore traditions. It has been suggested that because Max rushes to become white, Schuyler must have been an assimilationist.[24] But this is to miss the point of the book. Schuyler's satire attacks assimilationism. Actually Max is an archetypal black trickster who dons a white mask to "put on Ole Massa."[25]

Traditionally, the European *picaro* is a lovable rogue, a "rascal of low degree" who makes his way "more through his wits than his industry."[26] He never develops as a realistic character but "starts as a picaro and ends as a picaro, manifesting the same attitudes and qualities throughout."[27] He can be a trickster, for "tricks are essential to survival in chaos."[28] Reynard the Fox is the familiar European trickster, "pragmatic, unprincipled, resilient, solitary," a figure who "just manages to survive in his chaotic landscape, but who, in the ups and downs, can also put that world very much on the defensive."[29] Finally, the *picaro* is a "protean figure who can not only serve many masters but play different roles," wear different masks.[30]

There has been some debate about the derivation of the black American *picaro*. Black slaves brought to America tales of Ananse the Spider and Eshu the Yoruba trickster god. Once here they either created or adapted from existing folk motifs the Brer Rabbit stories. In these, as well as in the High John de Conquer tales, the more cunning creature was forced to match wits with a stronger but less quick-witted antagonist, whether it be Brer Wolf or Massa. In order to survive, the weaker creature quickly learned to "put on ole Massa." During the Harlem Renaissance, black scholars collected many of these tales; we can thank Arthur Huff Fauset and Zora Neale Hurston for making a body of folklore available for writers such as Schuyler.[31]

This is not to say that Schuyler had not encountered black *picaro*-trickster lore before he read the 1920s anthologies. During our May 1975 interview, he told me that he had been reared on Yankee versions of the black trickster: "There were *many* stories about black tricksters in the North," he told me. "They could be found in just about every town with a black population. I heard tales about High John de Conquer—Yankee style—long before I ever traveled in the South or read [Zora Neale] Hurston." He added that the word "hustler" is a much more descriptive term than "*picaro*" but that both words describe the type he had in mind when writing *Black No More*.

One other tradition should be noted. The Brer Rabbit and High John de Conquer tales are predominantly Southern and rural. At about the same time, however, the "sportin' life" trickster began to emerge as an urban (often Northern) folk hero. This trickster, "in the spirit of Brer Rabbit, became a credible underdog who could con his way to victory against heavy odds and symbolize the dream of escape from drudgery."[32] Both Seldom Seen and Max are "sportin' life" trickster-*picaros*.

In the person of Max are combined all of the characteristics of the *picaro*-trickster.[33] He is low born, naturally clever, amoral, obviously allergic to "honest" work. He desires money, women, and power. He "passes over" early, donning the white mask so that he can "put on Ole Massa." Like his folk predecessors he must live by his wits.

We first meet Max in Harlem. He is a "tall, dapper and smooth coffee-brown" man (17), one of the "gay blades of black Harlem" (19), a definite lady's man who lives for more and more amours. He is "shiekish" (22). Also he has a "slightly satanic cast" (17), a "sardonic twinkle" in his eye (42), and a "mephistophelian manner" (190).

One reason Max turns white is so that he can go to Atlanta and find Helen. But he has other motives that are more typically *picaro*.

He looks forward to "glorious new adventures" (46, 48) once he acquires the "necessary passport" of a white skin. He decides that "he would just play around, enjoy life and *laugh at the white folks up his sleeve*" (48; my italics). His desire to "laugh" at the white man is underscored by a recurrent dream: "[He] dreamed of sitting beside her [Helen] on a golden throne while millions of *manacled white slaves* prostrated themselves before him" (24; my italics).

As he assumes his new identity, Max's attitude toward whites is further defined.[34] When he leaves Crookman's sanitarium, a white woman reporter tries to interview him; he refuses to say a word until her newspaper pays him one thousand dollars and she agrees to "do the town with him" (38). When he arrives in Atlanta, he quickly notes the "hard, materialistic, grasping, in-bred society of whites" (63): "The unreasoning and illogical color prejudice of most of the people with whom he was forced to associate infuriated him. He often laughed cynically when some coarse, ignorant white man voiced his opinion concerning the inferior mentality and morality of the Negroes . . ." (63–64). This anger, tempered by cynicism, makes Max the perfect con artist. He feels no pity, especially when he realizes that each white character he encounters is stupid and greedy for money and/or power. In effect, Max is successful in sabotaging the South because he understands his adversaries' weaknesses and feels no qualms about exploiting them. His career is one long "secret mocking laugh" at the white establishment that never suspects Max is a black man in a white skin.

He soon realizes that the "Negro Menace" will serve as his "veritable gold mine" (65). He promptly smooth-talks his way into the Reverend Givens' confidence. Later he harangues the Knights of Nordica about the "menace," becomes their Grand Exalted Giraw, and succeeds in marrying their leader's daughter. He makes his first million dollars by speaking and writing on the "Menace" and the insidious Black-No-More, Inc. Then he uses the knights "as a stepladder to the real money" (71).

Teaming up with a newly whitened Bunny, Max sets out to milk Southern labor and business of as much money as possible. When labor becomes restless, Max publishes *The Warning,* "an eight-page newspaper carrying lurid red headlines and poorly-drawn . . . cartoons" which "the noble Southern working people" purchase and devour:

Matthew, in 14-point, one-syllable word editorials painted terrifying pictures of the menace confronting white supremacy and the utter necessity of

crushing it. . . . Very cleverly he linked up the Pope, the Yellow Peril, the
Alien Invasion and Foreign Entanglements with Black-No-More as devices
of the Devil (106).

For businessmen, Max paints a horrible picture of the dangers of
"Bolshevism, Socialism, Communism, Anarchism, trade unionism,
and other subversive movements" (108); in exchange for "contributions," Max promises "the perpetuation of Southern prosperity by
the stabilization of industrial relations" (108). When poor white
workers (most of whom are knights) in one Southern business
prepare to strike for better working conditions, Max and Bunny first
blackmail the two German managers for fifteen thousand dollars ("If
you don't come across I'll put the whole power of my organization
behind your hands. Then it'll cost you a hundred grand to get back
to normal" [122]), then spread rumors that the leaders of the strike
are really "whitened niggers." The laborers immediately turn on
each other, deciding that they are "far more interested in what they
considered, or were told was, the larger issue of race" (131).

As they become richer and more powerful, Max and Bunny
inevitably turn to politics. Again capitalizing on Southern prejudice,
they get Givens and Snobbcraft nominated. They obviously have
visions of greater fortunes and perhaps cabinet posts as they prepare
to manipulate the national election. That they come close to effect-
ing a Democratic victory attests to their skill as tricksters.

When research reveals that half of America has "tainted" blood
(and that most lily white Southern politicans are really "niggers"),
lynch law goes into effect. But Max and Bunny escape unscathed
with their women, the overflowing coffers of the Knights of
Nordica—and the last laugh: "He hated to leave. He had had such a
good time since he'd been white: plenty of money, almost unlimited
power, a beautiful wife, good liquor, and the pick of damsels within
reach" (185).

However, though he changes his skin color and works within
white racist organizations, Max never forgets that he is a black
trickster opposing the white man. At one point, Bunny says: "You
know, sometimes I forget who we are." And Max replies:

"Well, I don't. I know I'm a darky and I'm always on the alert"
(138). White prejudice makes this wily trickster's job easy. When
addressing the knights, Max "quickly saw that these people would
believe anything that was shouted at them loudly and convincingly
enough" (77–78). Elsewhere he says to Bunny:

"Bunny, I've learned something on this job, and that is that hatred and prejudice always go over big. These people have been raised on the Negro problem, they're used to it, they're trained to react to it. Why should I rack my brain to hunt up something else when I can use a dodge that's always delivered the goods?" (137)

Even the exchanges of the two *picaros* are traditional black asides about the white man. At one point, Bunny says admiringly to Max: "Gee, you've got educated since you've been down here with these crackers," and Max responds: "You flatter them, Bunny" (116). Later, Bunny asks what a "Grand Exalted Giraw" is, and Max answers that it doesn't matter, "the longer and sillier the title, the better the yaps like it" (121). Givens himself pays Max the supreme if ironic compliment when he says to Senator Kretin (in the presence of Max and Bunny): "If he [Max] can't do it, ain't nobody can. Him and Bunny here is as shrewd as some o' them old time darkies. He! He! He!" (136).

In typical picaresque fashion, Max never really develops as a character. Whenever a situation occurs that threatens Max's *picaro* role, Schuyler quickly intervenes. The story might have taken an entirely different turn, for example, if Max's occasional longings to return to the black world had won out. But each time Max contemplates his former life, his sorrow is forgotten when he realizes the enjoyment he is having as an adventurer. Early in the novel, Givens becomes jealous of Max's popularity (110–111), but when Max marries Helen and becomes Givens' son-in-law, Givens is "overjoyed . . . and . . . saw no clouds on the horizon" (111). Toward the end of the novel, even Snobbcraft begins to suspect that Max is not really white, but too late to expose him.

At only one point does Max step out of character and become a romantic (or melodramatic) hero. When Helen gives birth to a black baby, Max decides he must reveal his identity and take his chances. Just as he prepares to confess, Givens runs in to announce that the press has revealed *his* "tainted blood." Givens and Helen automatically assume that the color of the baby is the result of the Givens' blood line. Max, however, insists on making a completely gratuitous confession. Unrealistic as it is that a *picaro* would ever reveal himself, it is quickly apparent that Max has still not endangered himself.[35] Helen still loves him, Givens insists that "we're all niggers now," and the family happily flees the country just ahead of the lynch mob. A potentially tragic ending is averted, and we last see Max (with Givens and Helen and the baby) suntanning himself

at Cannes; he is trying to become just "as dusky" as the rest of the
nation (222).

Other than this brief lapse, Max plays the role of black *picaro* to
perfection, out-tricking the white man and turning racism against
itself; he creates chaos among his victims and adventure and fortune
for himself. Brer Rabbit or High John de Conquer would have been
proud.

III   *Rhetorical Devices: From Irony to Despair*

Schuyler employed a number of traditional satiric devices in
Black No More.[36] We have already seen that he uses *reductio ad
absurdum*, projection, caricature, parody, and a picaresque hero.
What adds spice is his use of rhetorical devices, his sustained irony,
and his ability to walk that fine line between Horatian lightheartedness and Juvenalian despair.

Schuyler is not above using many of the common forms of
humor.[37] For instance he loves puns and double entendres. Dr.
Napoleon Wellington Jackson (probably the NAACP's James Weldon Johnson) is famous for addressing groups of "sex-starved matrons who yearned to help the Negro stand erect" (93). A fine series
of double entendres occurs in Schuyler's description of the Reverend
McPhule, the white fundamentalist preacher whose love of God is
matched only by his sexual appetite: "When the men were at work
in the fields, the Man of God would visit house after house and
comfort the womenfolk with his Christian message. Being a
bachelor, he made these professional calls with great frequency"
(207). McPhule also receives women in his cabin, "the majority of
[whom] were middle-aged wives and adenoidal and neurotic girls."
"None," we are solemnly informed, "departed unsatisfied" (207).

Schuyler also, as we have seen, delights in *reductio ad absurdum*,
which he uses in individual scenes as well as at the beginning of
Black No More. For example, he satirizes all researchers who
specialize in trivia in the characters of Dr. Buggerie, Dr. Joseph
Bonds, and Professor Handen Moutthe, whose "projects" cannot
help but recall the Projectors in *Gulliver's Travels*. Handen
Moutthe is an "eminent anthropologist" and author of *The Sex Life
of Left-Handed Morons among the Ainus* (220). Buggerie is famous
for *The Incidence of Psittacosis among the Hiphopa Indians of the
Amazon Valley and Its Relation to Life Insurance Rates in the
United States* (197) and for *Putting Wasted Energy to Work* "in

which he called attention, by elaborate charts and graphs, to the possibilities of harnessing the power generated by the leaves of trees rubbing together on windy days" (156). Dr. Bonds is "engaged in a most vital and necessary work: i.e., collecting bales of data to prove satisfactorily to all that more money was needed to collect more data" (97).

Perhaps the most amusing single example of *reductio ad absurdum* occurs when Schuyler describes a presidential commission appointed by President Goosie to investigate the machinations of Black-No-More, Inc. The commission is appointed just before the election, and as Goosie has already been amply funded by Black-No-More, Inc., the commission exists more for the purpose of temporarily silencing public outrage than actually investigating the organization. After stalling twenty-four weeks, the commission finally issues a "preliminary report," recommending

stricter observance of the law, minor changes in the marriage laws, the organization of special matrimonial courts with trained genealogists attached to each, better equipped judges, more competent district attorneys, the strengthening of the Mann Act, the abolition of the road house, the closer supervision of dance halls, a stricter censorship on books and moving pictures and government control of cabarets (151).

This document, comprising 1,789 pages, is read by exactly nine people in the United States (152). Its recommendations, which do not even touch on the issue of Black-No-More, appear too late to affect the course of history.

Two other rhetorical devices that Schuyler uses to deflate his characters are antithesis and anticlimax. Antithesis involves yoking two dissimilar ideas in a compound sentence. Dr. Bonds, for example, "wanted work, not charity; but for himself he was always glad to get the charity with as little work as possible" (97). Here the words "work" and "charity" are employed to achieve ironic effect. Similar irony occurs in a description of Givens: "Not only had [he] toiled diligently to increase the prestige, power and membership of the defunct Klan, but he had also been a very hard worker in withdrawing as much money from its treasury as possible" (67–68).

Anticlimax, akin to antithesis, occurs when the satirist strings a series of descriptive words or phrases together, all of which work off the same syntactic structure; the first two (or three) words are usually serious, but the final word or phrase deflates. For example, a

Knights of Nordica choir sings a hymn "earnestly, vociferously and badly" (76). Bishop Whooper is "sixty, corpulent and an expert at the art of making cuckolds" (98). The members of the presidential commission "took hundreds of depositions, examined hundreds of witnesses and drank large quantities of liquor" (151). And Senator Kretin is "an incomparable Negro-baiter, a faithful servitor of his . . . state and the lusty father of several black families" (135).

It becomes apparent as we read *Black No More* that Schuyler is a master of irony, at having his characters say things that are the opposite of what Schuyler really thinks. In the preface Schuyler appears to praise the progress toward assimilationism that he really despises. His anticlimatic and antithetical structures indirectly condemn, as do his numerous caricatures and parodies. Dr. Beard is the kind of race "leader" that Schuyler fought constantly. The description of Mrs. Givens is typically ironic:

Mrs. Givens was a Christian. There was no doubt about it because she freely admitted it to everbody, with or without provocation. Of course she often took the name of the creator in vain when she got to quarreling with Henry; she had the reputation among her friends of not always stating the exact truth; she hated Negroes; her spouse had made bitter and profane comments concerning her virginity on their wedding night; and as head of the ladies' auxiliary of the defunct Klan she had copied her husband's financial methods; but that she was a devout Christian no one doubted (73).

As an ironist Schuyler walks the thin line between gentle lightheartedness and despair. In a single scene he can be both gently chiding and vicious. Yet as the book progresses and we move among the more obnoxious Southern fanatics, he becomes steadily more venomous until, in the penultimate scene, his rage triumphs. That savagery of tone so evident in the fourth book of *Gulliver's Travels*, in the last verses of *The Dunciad*, and in the "Eternal Rome" segment of *Catch-22* dominates *Black No More's* final chapters. The key scene is the Happy Hill episode.

This episode is about a lynching. Two Southern politicians have fled the mob in Atlanta that wishes to spill their "tainted" blood. One of the men is Arthur Snobbcraft, until recently a vice-presidential candidate. With him is Dr. Buggerie, the researcher who undertook to determine the racial purity of America. The two men try to flee the country by plane but crash in Mississippi. Knowing that the entire country is searching for them (and that Mississippi is perhaps the most dangerous state of all) Snobbcraft and Buggerie coat themselves with shoe polish before striking out in search of aid. Buggerie explains to his companion: "real niggers are scarce now and nobody would think of bothering a couple of them, even in Mississippi." In fact, "they'd probably be a curiosity" (200). Neither man, however, had ever encountered the citizens of Happy Hill. They have never tolerated "niggers." Their method of discouraging "blackamoors who sought the hospitality of the town was simple: the offending Ethiopian was either hung or shot or broiled" (204). But now that there were no more blacks, there "was nothing left to stimulate them but the old time religion and the clandestine sex orgies" (204–205).

Spiritual mentor to this "happy throng" is the Reverend McPhule, founder of the True Faith Christ Lovers' Church.[38] He has established a grotesque religion comprised of equal doses of fiery religion and sexual group-ins. McPhule aspires to establish the "truth" in every member of the community (there are still a few backward Methodists and Baptists); he feels "jealousy and ambition surge up within him" (208) whenever he passes one of the competing churches. Filled with "holy zeal," he prays for a sign from heaven, knowing that the best way to win the entire community is to have "the Lord . . . send him a nigger for his congregation to lynch! That would, indeed, be marked evidence of [his] power" (208).

Buggerie and Snobbcraft, their faces and arms covered with black shoe polish, stumble onto the scene in the midst of a revival. They are set upon joyfully: "The Sign! Look! Niggers! Praise God!" (208). The men gain a brief respite when they reveal that they are not really black. But a villager arrives with a newspaper that prominently features pictures of Snobbcraft and Buggerie and announces that they are "niggers." "The Lord's will be done," screams McPhule, and his "flock" prepares for an old-fashioned lynching.

The lynching itself is a horrible parody of a true religious celebration: "The two men . . . were stripped naked, held down by husky and willing farm hands and their ears and genitals cut off with jack knives amid the fiendish cries of men and women. . . . Some wag sewed their ears to their backs and they were released and told to run" (216). Revolvers crack, the fleeing men are brought down "amid the uproarious laughter of the congregation" (217) and prepared for the final sacrifice. They are bound together to a stake, and "little boys and girls *gaily* gather excelsior, scrap paper, twigs and small branches while their *proud* parents fetched logs, boxes, kerosene . . ." (217; my italics).

McPhule delivers a "benediction" and lights the pyre; as the flame brings screams of pain from the victims, the "crowd whooped with glee and Reverend McPhule beamed with satisfaction" (217). The ghastly ceremony reaches its climax:

The odor of cooking meat permeated the clear, country air and many a nostril was guiltily distended. . . . When the roasting was over, the more adventurous members of Rev. McPhule's *flock* rushed to the stake and groped in the two bodies for *skeletal souvenirs* such as forefingers, toes and teeth. *Proudly* their *pastor* looked on. This was the crowning of a life's ambition. . . . *God had answered his prayers* (217–18; my italics).

The crowning irony occurs as the "flock" dances around the pyre. In the crowd "there were two or three whitened Negroes, who, remembering what their race had suffered in the past, would fain have gone to the assistance of the two men," but "fear for their own lives restrained them. Even so they were looked at rather sharply by some of the Christ Lovers because they did not appear to be enjoying the spectacle as thoroughly as the rest" (218). Noting the suspicious looks, the two ex-blacks "began to yell and prod the burning bodies with sticks and cast stones at them." This has the expected result: "This exhibition restored them to favor and banished any suspicion that they might not be *one-hundred-per-cent Americans*" (218; my italics). This single episode reveals Schuyler at his satiric best. He has become the compleat misanthrope, lashing out savagely, if futilely, against an evil that is all the more horrifying because it exists in a "religious" and "patriotic" community. All human values have been subverted. In fifteen pages, Schuyler evokes the despair that wrung these lines from Pope in *The Dunciad:*

> Religion blushing veils her sacred fires.
> And unawares morality expires.
> For public flame, nor private, dares to shine;
> Nor human spark is left, nor glimpse divine!
> Lo! thy dread empire, CHAOS! is restored . . .
> And universal darkness buries all.[39]

IV   *Themes: Despair And Hope*

The Happy Hill episode is so bitter that we are left with a sense of despair. Chaos reigns supreme. Yet there is a faint glimmering of hope in *Black No More.*

Satire has a dual purpose. It attacks, on the one hand, ridiculing man's folly and vice. Most of a satire is devoted to this attack. But buried somewhere in the invective is the satirist's message to his fellow man. The satirist begins, notes W. O. S. Sutherland, by establishing "a contrast in values": "The author creates one set of values to act as a criterion; the other [set] is the subject of the satire. The degree to which the criterion is obvious varies sharply from work to work; often it exists only by implication. But it must be present."[40]

Schuyler the universal pessimist has already been examined. In brief, he presents us in *Black No More* with a stark picture of two societies, one white, one black. The first is convinced that "White is Right" and is willing to use any form of oppression necessary to dominate the minority. The second has been conditioned to believe that "White is Right" and thus tries in one way or another to assimilate into the majority. Given these two societies, it does not take too much imagination to figure out what might happen if an organization such as Black-No-More, Inc. tried to rob white society of its minority race. America, Schuyler projects, would go berserk. Politicians would harangue their followers about the "menace," big business would tremble, supremacist organizations would proliferate. Men like McPhule would become the "white hopes," the anti-Christs who seek out and lynch the hated white "niggers." This would be done, of course, in the name of Christianity and patriotism.

Though *Black No More* is a very pessimistic novel, it also has its more hopeful moments. The key to locating Schuyler's positive messages is to read his irony correctly, keeping in mind that irony traditionally is the device whereby an author's "actual intent is expressed in words which carry the opposite meaning."[41] Schuyler does not recommend hair straighteners or skin whiteners, for example, even if his satire suggests that he does. He does not want us to think that Mrs. Givens is a model Christian, though he says she is. He never intends for us to believe for a moment that a fool like Dr. Buggerie is really capable of brilliant monographs.

So scattered throughout *Black No More* are passages that recommend their opposite. Some are more obvious than others. For example, if we know that Schuyler was enraged during the 1920s by the exploitation of the average working man, we cannot miss the significance of a little passage the author sneaks into the middle of the book. It begins when the Republican and Democratic leaders become worried that the disappearance of blacks will cause irreparable harm to the nation's political structure. The leaders realize that the "upper classes" may soon lose control of their "docile, contented Anglo-Saxon laborers" (134). They fear "widespread revolt against the existing medieval industrial conditions and [the] resultant reduction of profits and dividends" (134). Worse things may follow. "Mill barons" may "have to do away with child labor" (134). Laborers may "soon forsake . . . both the parties and go . . . socialist" (134). This, in turn, leads to horrible visions of

old-age pensions, eight-hour laws, unemployment insurance, workingmen's compensation, minimum-wage legislation, abolition of child labor, dissemination of birth-control information, monthly vacations for prospective mothers . . . with pay, and the probable killing of individual initiative and incentive by taking the ownership of national capital out of the hands of two million people and putting it into the hands of one hundred and twenty million (135).

Can there be any question about Schuyler's true feelings?

But Schuyler does not limit himself to this message of socialism. There is definite evidence in *Black No More* that he also wanted to make his black readers aware of their heritage and proud of their color. At one point, after lying-in hospitals are established for expectant mothers concerned about the color of *new children,* the narrator slyly notes that there were a few "mulatto babies whose mothers, *charmed by the beautiful color of their offspring,* had defied convention and not turned them white" (132; my italics). At another point the narrator informs us that, while most of the black population had rushed to become white, there remained "a couple of thousand diehards who refuse[d] to give up their color" (158). Elsewhere Crookman's associate, Hank Johnson, sadly announces that "Ah aint seen a brown-skin ooman [woman] in so long Ah doan know whut Ah'd do if I seen one" (158).

Even the supposedly amoral Bunny admits near the end of the novel that all along he has loved "a sweet Georgia brown":

"She must be the last black gal in the country," Matthew remarked, glancing *enviously* at his friend. "How come she didn't get white, too?"

"Well," Bunny replied, *a slight hint of pride* in his voice. "She's a *race patriot.* She's funny that way" (195; my italics).

Significant also is Helen's transformation. The woman who once refused to dance with "niggers" in a Harlem nightclub learns that she has "tainted blood"—but only after she has married (and loved)

Max and given birth to his child. When Max confesses that he is really black, Helen realizes that "there was no feeling of revulsion at the thought that her husband was a Negro. . . . They had money and a beautiful, brown baby. . . . To hell with the world! To hell with society!" (193–94). Her attitudes on race have changed drastically, and her conversion may be seen as another example of Schuyler's hope for the future.

Max's attitude is important, too. Throughout the novel he feels longings (momentary though they are) for the black world he has left behind. For example, soon after he passes over, he visits a white cabaret and "found it pretty dull":

There was something lacking in these ofay places of amusement, or else there was something present that one didn't find in . . . Harlem. The joy and abandon here was obviously forced. Patrons went to extremes to show each other they were having a wonderful time. It was all so strained (40).

Max realizes what is missing: "The Negroes . . . were much gayer, enjoyed themselves more deeply and yet they were more restrained, actually more refined" (40). He becomes aware of the "lumbering [white] couples" on the dance floor, whom he compares to the black couples who "followed the rhythm accurately, effortlessly and with easy grace." White couples, he notes in a grotesque image, were "out of step half the time and working as strenuously as stevedores emptying the bowels of a freighter, . . . noisy, awkward, inelegant" (40). Max feels "a momentary pang of mingled disgust, disillusionment and nostalgia" (40):

[He] felt at home here among these black folk. Their jests, scraps of conversation and lusty laughter all seemed like heavenly music. Momentarily he felt a disposition to stay among them, to share again their troubles which they seemed always to bear with a lightness that was not indifference (46).

In Atlanta, where he still feels vague longings for the black world (63), he learns about whites. He finds them "pretty dull," and "little different from Negroes, except that they were uniformly less courteous and less interesting" (63):

He was moving in white society now and he could compare it with the society he had known as a Negro. . . . What a let-down it was from the good-breeding, sophistication, refinement and gentle cynicism to which he had become accustomed as a popular young man about town in New York's Black Belt (63–64).

Max is cynical and clever enough to understand white society and to exploit it. But Dr. Crookman, the discoverer of the Black-No-More process, is not. *Black No More* is also the story of Dr. Crookman's initiation into reality.

Something of a black Beelzebub who kills blackness and gives birth to whiteness, Crookman is, in the final analysis, a classic *naif*.[42] An "ebony black man" (26) of poor parents who "boasted that they belonged to the Negro aristocracy" (54), Crookman as a youth was protected "from the defeatist psychology so prevalent among American Negroes" (54). He was sheltered from the "crudity, coarseness and cruelty of life" (54), so he grew up an idealist, "above all . . . a great lover of his race" though he had no real knowledge about it (55). He faithfully "studied its history, read of its struggles and kept up with its achievements" (55). He "subscribed to black publications and had a collection of African and black American art" (55). He becomes, in short, "wedded to everything black except the black woman—his wife was a white girl with remote Negro ancestry . . ." (55).[43] As he returns to America with his remarkable "process," Crookman sees himself as a black messiah:

He saw in his great discovery the solution to the most annoying problem in American life. Obviously, he reasoned, *if there were no Negroes, there could be no Negro problem*, and Americans could concentrate their attention on something more constructive. Through his efforts . . . it would be possible to do what agitation, education and legislation had failed to do (54–55; my italics).

Of course, Schuyler the satirist must ridicule Crookman's attitude, even though Schuyler the man certainly agrees that racial distinctions are absurd. A few lines later, Crookman learns of the opposition to his work:

He was naively surprised that there should be opposition to his work. Like most men with a vision, a plan, a program or a remedy, he fondly imagined people to be intelligent enough to accept a good thing when it was offered to them, which was conclusive evidence that *he knew little about the human race* (55; my italics).

Crookman succeeds to some extent in proving his point because he

helps over ten million black Americans "pass over." But his naivete
emerges in the end when he releases a monograph announcing that
ex-blacks are two or three shades lighter than whites. Obviously he
expects white America to be momentarily surprised, then laugh
heartily at his magnificent hoax. Instead, America almost immediately becomes "enthusiastically mulatto-minded" and sets out
to become as black as possible, in the process setting up the same
old discrimination laws. The status quo has been restored, but now
whites are the "nigger" class. Only then does Crookman realize the
intensity of America's "colorphobia." His final reaction is muted, yet
revealing; seeing a photograph of Max and his family trying to
become as dark as possible on the beaches at Cannes, Crookman
"smiled wearily" (222). At this point Crookman has been initiated
into reality.

If Crookman learns the truth about America's "unreasoning and
illogical color prejudice" (66) belatedly, Schuyler knew the truth
before he began to write *Black No More*. Throughout his career he
preached Crookman's message, but as a satirist he knew that
attempting to make America act sensibly was futile.

V *Critical Response*

At first *Black No More* was received quite favorably. Black critics
praised the overall effect while criticizing its literary flaws. Most of
them seemed in agreement with Arthur P. Davis, who said that the
work "was an excellent first novel."[44]

Thus W. E. B. Du Bois announced that it was "an extremely
significant work" which would be "abundantly misunderstood" because "the writer of satire . . . is always misunderstood by the
simple."[45] The dean of black American letters, Alain Locke, said
that *Black No More* "was significant," that Schuyler "has a theme
worthy of satire," and that his work succeeded because "of the
novelty and the potential power of the satiric attack on the race
problem." Locke concluded that "one of the great veins of Negro
fiction has been opened."[46] Sterling A. Brown noted that "the
idealism seen in the apologetic, the bourgeois, and the 'passing'
novels found a gleeful critic in George Schuyler," and that *Black No
More*, though "farce rather than satire," was "refreshingly different."[47] Arthur P. Davis argued that the novel "thoroughly and
ironically dissected most of the national foibles and weaknesses of

Americans black and white," and concluded that Schuyler was "refreshingly devoid of the 'racial' cant which so often creeps into the writings of 'our' people."[48] Fellow-satirist Rudolph Fisher praised Schuyler's "commendable effort," in which "the idea is large and suggestive, the general plan adequate, the movement swift and direct, and the climaxes satisfyingly inevitable."[49] None of these critics questioned Schuyler's racial loyalties.

Neither did early white critics, with the exception of Dorothy Van Doren. The reviewer for *The New York Times*, for example, said that *Black No More* was "a fairly amusing satire on the subject of color," though it lacked originality and was overwritten.[50] H. L. Mencken said that while the work "is amusing," its attack on black leaders was sometimes "uncomfortably savage."[51] But Dorothy Van Doren carried Mencken's hint of disapproval to ridiculous lengths: "Perhaps the Negro will never write great literature while he tries to write white literature," she said: "it may be that [the Negro writer] can express himself only by music and rhythm, and not by words."[52] Having resurrected the "natural rhythm" thesis, Van Doren gave her verdict: Mr. Schuyler had produced poor "white satire"—a term she never defined.

More recently, variations on the Van Doren thesis have been set forth by a few white critics, including Robert Bone and Charles Larson. Bone does admit that Harlem Renaissance "satire reaches its highest development in George Schuyler's *Black No More* and Wallace Thurman's *Infants of the Spring*."[53] But then he argues that Schuyler's novel is "assimilationist" (as opposed to nationalistic) and reveals its author's "urge to whiteness," his "denial of racial . . . identity," his "revulsion toward the Negro masses," his "desire to behave like a white person—and a middle-class white person at that."[54] According to Bone, Schuyler desired "to abandon ethnic ties and identify with the dominant white majority."[55] Like other Harlem Renaissance satire Schuyler's, "though often directed against whites, is predominatly self-satire," having "psychological roots in assimilation."[56] Charles Larson, on the other hand, wrote the introduction for the 1971 edition of the novel. In it he argues that Schuyler's thesis is that "the New Negro will be white or nothing at all."[57] *Black No More* demonstrates no "pride in being black" but is "a plea for assimilation, for mediocrity, for reduplication, for faith in the (white) American dream" (12). Larson, like Bone, buttresses his argument with quotations from "The Negro-Art Hokum" (he cites the "lampblacked Anglo-Saxon" reference) and from *Black and Conservative,* thereby attempting to show that Schuyler has always marched to "the sounds of a different drummer" (13). The impression Larson leaves is that he just does not like Schuyler. Whether or not this is true, he tends to judge *Black No More* (as Bone does) out of context and according to a preconceived theory. Neither man discusses Schuyler as *satirist;* they are more concerned with his politics and racial integrity.

The Van Doren-Bone-Larson interpretation of *Black No More* has held sway during the 1960s and 1970s. A few critics have looked again at *Black No More* and speculated along more Du Boisian lines. The late Janheinz Janz, for example, after noting that the Harlem Renaissance "was bound to end in satire," praised "the great satire by George Schuyler . . . which reduced 'ad absurdum' the whole race question."[58] Ruth Miller stated that Schuyler's novel "reflects the breadth of his experience," has "a panoramic sweep, drawn in the style of a Marx Brothers' film," and "ends in the only lynching I have read that is humorous."[59] Carl Milton Hughes claimed that the novel is "one of the most scathing attacks upon American color phobia to be found in American literature."[60]

But most critics, be they black or white, now ignore Schuyler, after paying lip service to his historical significance. The reissue of *Black No More* in 1971 sparked a few critical statements but no in-depth analyses. Only Arthur P. Davis has recognized that Schuyler is more significant than others realize; Davis devoted a chapter to the man in *From the Dark Tower.*[61]

Actually these critics are being upstaged by a growing body of writers and scholars who regularly flout literary conventions set down by establishment critics. These rebels are the science fiction writers of America, and they are more than willing to claim Schuyler as a kindred spirit. One of our most popular black writers, Ishmael Reed, instructed us all in 1973 when he flatly insisted that *Black No More* "was the first science fiction novel written by an Afro-American."[62] Two years later, John Pfeiffer, writing in the prestigious *Extrapolation,* claimed that Schuyler's Swiftian satire ranks among the very best works of speculative fiction. Pfeiffer even made the point, stressed throughout this chapter, that *Black No More's* underlying message is that "Black is beautiful."[63] And a year later Ivor A. Rogers, while discussing the golden age of American SF in the 1920s and 1930s, commented that *Black No More* "is a well-written and ironic commentary on racial relations" in the United States, that it has been "unfairly forgotten," and that it is "a superior work."[64] As of this writing, scholars are writing dissertations and presenting papers on the contributions of authors like Schuyler to the field of science fiction. It would be a great irony if the world of science fiction, itself often looked down upon by establishment writers, proved that *Black No More* is indeed an American classic.

CHAPTER 6

Black Muckraker: Slaves Today

I F *Black No More* is the first extended satire by a black American,
Slaves Today: A Story of Liberia is the first African novel by a
black American. It signaled Schuyler's emergence as a top-notch
international investigative reporter: "It was the first time," Schuyler
said later, "that anything like this had happened to a Negro newspaperman."[1] The novel generated a considerable amount of controversy, but Schuyler always maintained that he told the story as
honestly as he could.[2]

At the end of 1930, probably while reading page proofs for *Black
No More,* Schuyler received a call from George Palmer Putnam,
who was engaged in establishing the firm of Brewer, Warren, and
Putnam. Putnam asked Schuyler to undertake a secret mission to
investigate charges of slavery brought against the Liberian government by the League of Nations. Aside from Putnam, Schuyler's
wife, Julian Mason (the editor of the *New York Evening Post,* which
was arranging for the publication and syndication of the Liberian
articles), and Arthur Spingarn at the NAACP, no one was to know
about Schuyler's real mission. Ostensibly he was going first to
England to investigate British cooperatives (he was then trying to
establish his own Young Negroes' Cooperative League) and then on
to Liberia for a vacation. He left the following January, arrived in
Monrovia in February, toured much of the country, conducted a
series of interviews with everyone from local chieftains to the
president of Liberia, contracted a severe case of malaria, and
returned to New York in late May. There he wrote and subsequently published "Slavery in Liberia" in major white papers
(*New York Evening Post, Buffalo Express, Philadelphia Public
Ledger,* and *The Washington Post*) in June and July and in several
Negro newspapers (including his own *Pittsburgh Courier*) in September and October. The series was syndicated by the Capital News
Service. Finally, in October 1931, Brewer, Warren, and Putnam
published *Slaves Today.*

I *The Background*

Liberia was founded by freed black American slaves in 1822 and achieved independence in 1847. The ruling class, those whom Schuyler calls Americo-Liberians, were descendants of the American slaves; the "bush" (hinterland) natives were indigenous Africans. During World War I, the Americo-Liberian government in Monrovia found itself desperately in need of money and apparently agreed to sell "laborers," which it had recruited forcibly from the bush, to the Spanish government at fifty dollars per laborer. The Spanish, in turn, imported these slaves to the plantations of Fernando Po, a Spanish island off the coast of Nigeria. Any bush recruits not sold to the Spanish were apparently doled out to members of the ruling class as servants or as concubines, depending on their age and sex. The whole matter was kept fairly quiet until 1929, when J. R. F. Faulkner, head of the People's Party, exposed the matter during a lecture tour in the United States; he further complained that a recent presidential election in which he had been a candidate had been rigged by the ruling Whig Party so that he would lose. Various international commissions investigated Faulkner's charges between 1929 and 1931; token changes were made by the Whig government (including the banishment of the "Spanish Connection" but not of domestic slavery, according to Schuyler); and Edwin Barclay, another Whig, assumed the presidency after another election. Various missionary groups continued to turn a deaf ear on the complaints of men like Faulkner; and the Firestone Company, which had contracted with the Liberian government to set up rubber plantations in 1925, practiced either an enlightened or an oppressive influence, depending on who was telling the tale (the League of Nations' Commission and Schuyler exonerated Firestone). When Schuyler returned to New York in 1931 and announced in his columns that slavery was still being practiced in Liberia, that the missionaries were doing nothing to stop political corruption and servitude (and in fact were silently sanctioning them), that Firestone was one of the few true voices of moderation in Liberia, and that the only thing that could save Liberia was the defeat of the Whig Party and the election of Liberia's Abraham Lincoln (Faulkner)—when he presented all of this in a series of eight sensational articles, the whole controversy over Liberia (and the sending of Schuyler to investigate the situation) erupted anew. Though the U. S. State Department made the right noises, nothing concrete was done about the Liberia situation, even after Schuyler's articles appeared.[3]

The Liberian matter and the reaction to Schuyler's articles must be viewed against the larger backdrop of the Harlem Renaissance.[4] During the 1920s Africa had become a matter of deep interest to black writers, artists, politicians, and race leaders. Marcus Garvey, the "Black Moses" of black America in the early 1920s, organized a "back to Africa" movement as part of his Universal Negro Improvement Association (UNIA). W. E. B. Du Bois organized four Pan-Africa congresses and wrote extensively about "Mother Africa." Many writers, including Alain Locke, Langston Hughes, Claude McKay, and Effie Lee Newsome, celebrated the African heritage. But few black personalities actually had the opportunity to visit Africa—Hughes, Du Bois, and Schuyler being the exceptions. Indeed, some have said that black writers were so desirous of tracing the African heritage that they overromanticized the motherland. It remained for Langston Hughes in "Afro-American Fragment" and Countee Cullen in "Heritage" to express some of the doubts thoughtful Renaissance writers were experiencing about the significance of Mother Africa for blacks three hundred years removed from her.

And it remained for Schuyler to deromanticize Africa completely; he insisted that Liberia—which had become in the 1920s more of a symbol than a real place—was just as flawed as any other society. By attacking Liberia, the oldest black republic in West Africa, by attacking its rulers and its missionaries, and by exonerating what many felt was the neocolonialism of Firestone—and by doing it all for a white newspaper chain and a white publishing company—Schuyler managed to arouse the hostility of numerous individuals and organizations (missionaries, Garveyites, black nationalists, etc.). It was said in not a few editorials and columns that Schuyler had not known all that much about Africa or Liberia to begin with and that he had been duped by the white man.[5] Such charges are debatable. Schuyler had carte blanche from Putnam and Mason. He undertook a dangerous secret mission (the Whig government never found out that Schuyler was investigating the slavery charges; he told me that if it had, he might have suffered a mysterious death in the hinterland[6]) for which he carefully prepared. And he produced a series of articles (and a novel) that are obviously based on sound investigative reporting. Indeed, the articles reveal that Schuyler knew as much about the subject as anyone writing on it. If he was the dupe of "white interests," then the hustle was a good one indeed, for

Schuyler worked hard to find out the facts—not only about governmental corruption and domestic slavery but about Firestone's interests, contributions, and overall role in Liberian politics.

II *Slavery in Liberia: The Articles*

Reading Schuyler's "Slavery in Liberia," we realize almost immediately that we are in the presence of a skilled muckraker, one of the band of journalists and novelists like Upton Sinclair who "searched out and exposed publicly real or apparent misconduct."[7] Schuyler devotes his first article[8] to sex and violence. He describes the fate of two chieftains who testified before the U.N. Commission that their villages had been looted and their people fired upon (the basis for one of the sequences in *Slaves Today*). He goes into some detail about one district commissioner who seized beautiful women for his harem (though Schuyler does not name the man, it is probably one Davis Carter who served as the model for David Jackson in *Slaves Today*) and then moves into a discussion of specific Americo-Liberians who maintained harems in Monrovia. In the first and second articles, Schuyler describes vividly the way little "pawns" (native boys in domestic slavery) were whipped into submission. In the fourth article, Schuyler compares the "upstanding" native with the "depraved" Americo-Liberian, and rhapsodizes on the beauties of the bush (this article anticipates several of the native scenes in *Slaves Today*):

Liberia is perhaps the most beautiful country in Africa. It is a great botanical and zoological garden where every tropical animal, tree, flower and fruit is to be found. . . . But its greatest wealth is its people. The aborigines are as admirable as most of their Americo-Liberian taskmasters are despicable. Everywhere in the hinterland one finds the natives self-supporting in every way, whereas their rulers are not. The native towns are uniformly clean and neat, and their inhabitants are generally honest, truthful and trustworthy.[9]

Describing the native division of labor according to skill and the artistic beauty and functionality of native handicrafts, Schuyler notes that "here is a perfectly organized and functioning society".[10] By way of contrast, in the same article Schuyler describes an interview he had with President Barclay and the manner in which he acquired nonsensitive material first (thus establishing some rapport), while saving the questions sure to arouse anger for the end of the interview; if he were expelled from the palace, he would still have some quotations for his series. The contrasts between bush and capital, between "upstanding" native and "wily" Americo-Liberian, would be emphasized again and again in the novel. To his credit, Schuyler's interview with Barclay is probing without being nasty.

In his next article, Schuyler describes his interview with W. D. Hines, resident manager of the Firestone plantation. Schuyler's obvious approval of Hines' businesslike manner probably prepared the way for charges of Schuyler's having sold out. Again, in Schuyler's defense, it should be noted that he double-checked his findings elsewhere and that Hines was able to demonstrate that Firestone had done much more than the missionaries or the Americo-Liberian government in the areas of education, in-service training, sanitation, fair wages, and the like—all of which obviously made a good impression on Schuyler's Yankee sense of efficiency. (It should also be noted that Schuyler—champion of the common man, in this case the native Liberian—extolled any man or organization that had the best interests of the workers in mind.)

In his sixth article, Schuyler launches a bitter (yet documented) attack on the American or American-trained missionaries, who did nothing to ease the plight of the native Liberian. They "stood with closed mouths" as the slave trade went on; he can only wonder "why there has never been an outburst of protest" against present conditions "from the missionaries who overrun the country." These "good Baptists, Methodists, Catholics, Lutherans and Episcopalians" who "come from the Land of the Free" not only do nothing about the slavery but continue to defend the present government. In the mission schools, the missionaries "educate" the very rulers who now enslave the natives; "whatever be the character and training of the Americo-Liberians, the missionaries are largely responsible."[11] This article obviously paved the way for the character of Henry Briggs, bishop of Liberia, in *Slaves Today.*

In his seventh article, Schuyler focuses on the economic disaster that was occurring in Liberia under the Whigs. In the final article, Schuyler concludes that Liberia "may" be redeemed if she cleans house and elects a shrewd businessman—namely, Faulkner who is not only a politician but a fellow newspaperman! Faulkner, like Lincoln, will set the slaves free, for he is a "dynamo of energy," an "avenging angel."[12]

III   Slaves Today: *The Plot*

Two narrative threads run through *Slaves Today*. The first is a
blunt and often satiric exposé of the entrenched Americo-Liberian
government which exploits the natives. The "Monrovia Thread" is
based directly on Schuyler's firsthand experiences in Liberia. The
second thread is a melodramatic account of two native victims—Zo,
who is sold into foreign slavery, and his new bride Pameta, who is
forced into domestic servitude in a harem. The "Zo-Pameta Thread"
interweaves with the "Monrovia Thread" so that both dramatize the
theme of man's inhumanity to man.

Internal references suggest that the action of the novel occurs
between 1928 and May 1931, when Barclay and the entrenched
Whig Party defeated Faulkner. Chapters One and Eleven envelop
the melodrama, and passages in Chapters Six, Nine and Ten develop the "Monrovia Thread."

The "Monrovia Thread" includes harsh pictures of Cooper
Johnson (Barclay or, perhaps, his predecessor), president and head
of the Conservative (Whig) Party; Sammy Williams, vice-president
and secret organizer of the Fernando Po slave trade; and John
Collins, the Spanish consul who, with Williams, collects and deports
the slaves. Another evil figure is David Jackson, whom President
Johnson appoints commissioner of the first district; it is Jackson's
duty to collect tribute from native villages and to find "boys" (slaves)
for Sammy Williams and John Collins. Jackson succeeds so well that
he is later appointed director of public works. Jackson's lieutenant
and eventual successor is the malignant Captain Burns. Finally,
the Right Reverend Henry Briggs, the bishop of Liberia, while not
as villainous and cruel as Jackson and Burns, is a hypocrite who
preaches Christianity yet defends a government that practices corruption and slavery. The church's role, he maintains at one point, is
to "bring the message of Jesus Christ to the heathen," not to become
involved in politics.[13]

Arrayed against the villains is a handful of reformers led by Tom
Saunders (Faulkner), another Americo-Liberian, who is a successful
businessman, the editor of the opposition "Liberian Liberal," and
head of the Liberal Party (People's Party). Saunders acquires help
toward the end of the novel through a somewhat weak character—
Rufus Henderson (the Conservative Party's attorney general)—who
becomes so enraged with the slave trade that he defects to the
Liberal Party.

In Chapter Two, we meet the native Liberians, represented by the Gola tribe in Takama. There Zo, the young and naive hero, is celebrating his marriage to the lovely Pameta, daughter of Chief Bongomo. During the festivities, the Golas are suddenly set upon by Commissioner Jackson and his Frontier Force. Because the necessary tribute to Monrovia is not forthcoming, Jackson orders the village chief beaten in public and then, when the outraged villagers attack his forces, shot. In order to teach the Golas a lesson, Jackson not only raises the tribute, but seizes Pameta for his harem. After Jackson leaves, Tolo, the native doctor, casts a spell on the commissioner so that he will die a violent death.

Zo pursues Jackson's forces and attempts to rescue his new bride. He is captured by Jackson's servants, sent to Monrovia, and sold to the Spanish. The central chapters in the book are the best, for in them Schuyler describes Zo's two year "tour of duty" on the island of Fernando Po under the Spanish. Zo's companion in hell is the worldly wise and somewhat cynical Soki, the character who speaks for Schuyler in the "Zo-Pameta Thread," just as Saunders speaks for Schuyler in the "Monrovia Thread."

As a slave, Zo not only works long hours but attempts an escape, is betrayed, becomes temporarily enamoured of a high class prostitute, and eventually becomes so sick with malaria that he must be sent to the infamous island hospital. There he sees horrible cases of yaws, yellow fever, smallpox, syphilis, and elephantiasis. Eventually cured and released, Zo serves out his tour. He is returned to Monrovia (without Soki, who suddenly snaps the last day on the island and attacks a guard), receives his pay, experiences with wide-eyed pleasure the fleshpots of Monrovia, and is finally arrested for disturbing the peace and fined his entire two year's salary. Still as naive and impetuous as ever, he finally returns to the bush to look for his bride. He finds Pameta lying discarded in the jungle, riddled with disease. As she dies in his arms, Zo vows to avenge her. He sneaks into Jackson's compound and slits the villain's throat, then is shot to death by a sentry.

Just as the "Zo-Pameta Thread" ends unhappily, so the "Monrovia Thread" ends on a note of despair. Saunders loses the presidential bid in a blatantly rigged election; the forces for progress are defeated throughout Liberia by the entrenched Conservative Party. The slave trade is not stopped but is moved further underground so that no snoopers will stumble upon it. Domestic slavery continues.

A number of things do not work well in *Slaves Today*. The characters are for the most part one dimensional: Jackson is the most obvious of villains, while Johnson and Williams are the evil forces behind him; the natives are all virtuous, as is Tom Saunders; Zo is the naive and idealistic hero; Pameta is the archetypal heroine, more sinned against than sinning. These characters could be moved into almost any other location and still function. Unfortunately, Schuyler rarely reverts to the kind of satire he is capable of; satire in several instances would have made the worst of villains and the best of heroes or heroines somewhat more tolerable. The only character who does not fall into the good-evil category is the weak bishop, though even he is more a stock hypocrite than a real person.

Though Schuyler labored hard on his two narrative threads, he only occasionally comes up with effective pieces of contrast (the filth of Monrovia in Chapter One is nicely contrasted with the wholesomeness of the Gola village and the jungle in Chapter Two) and is generally unable to unify the threads. Thus his "Monrovia Thread" is pure exposé with a dash of satire and his "Zo-Pameta Threat" is pure melodrama with no humor at all. There is too much philosophizing, too many set speeches, too many anticipated actions. The novel would have worked better if Schuyler had developed only one of the narrative threads and maintained the same tone throughout.

Specific details in the novel also cause problems for the reader. Tolo, the native doctor who casts a spell on Jackson, disappears entirely and the effectiveness (or lack of effectiveness) of his spell is never mentioned. Another character, the malevolent Joe, Jackson's manservant, also disappears from the story. Soki's sudden attack on the Fernando Po guard is out of character, for throughout he is the cool, rational cynic who would never let his emotions betray his desire to gain his freedom. And Zo, the young, lusty bridegroom who adores his wife, might occasionally forget his bride; but he would not continue to forget her while he dallied for several chapters in Monrovia. Schuyler so wanted to show the corruption of the judicial system that he almost bodily seized Zo and forced him into one scene after another, pitting the naive hero against the evil lawyers and judges. Finally, it is almost incomprehensible that the archvillain, Jackson, once he learns of Pameta's disease, would suddenly feel guilt! Perhaps he might have felt sorrow that he could no longer use her; perhaps he might have felt fear that he too was diseased. But guilt is totally inconsistent with his character.

Such inconsistencies and flaws suggest that Schuyler wrote too quickly and that he was primarily concerned with dramatizing the evils of the America-Liberian government.

There are several noteworthy characteristics, however. Schuyler obviously knows Liberia, both hinterland and big city, and he is quite adept at describing what it is like to walk through a jungle in the heat and humidity. He captures the sound of pidgin nicely, a trick many writers have attempted and failed. Schuyler's native scenes are consistently well done, and his compassion for and appreciation of tribal life is evident. The wedding scene in Chapter Two is especially good. The wealth of detail throughout the story could only have been provided by someone who had actually visited the African hinterland and seen a number of villages at work and play. Strangely, Schuyler's native scenes are consistently better than his Monrovia scenes; we might expect just the opposite from a muckraking journalist.

Even more interesting, Schuyler built the Fernando Po scenes on imagination alone. He had not visited the island, he probably never saw the slave trade in action, and he could not have had a very good idea of what it was like being a slave on a plantation. Obviously Schuyler obtained some very informative interviews with ex-slaves. The Fernando Po hospital scene alone is worth the whole book, and the story of the Fernando Po slave (Blackie) who escaped temporarily into the rugged mountains of the island is cleverly executed and vividly realized.

IV   Slaves Today: *Major Themes*

Slaves Today includes many of the same themes that appear in *Black No More.* In both novels, the evil characters are one dimensional, almost allegorical figures representing lust, greed, savagery, hypocrisy, and man's inhumanity to man. These universal evils are attacked and their opposite virtues—love, courage, dignity, integrity—are praised. Once again (as in *Black No More* and other pieces), Schuyler identifies with the common man against the entrenched power structure, with the young and militant against the old and corrupted.

As satirist and muckraker, Schuyler could not help but focus on the major irony of the Liberia story—supposedly "civilized" people exploiting supposedly "savage" people, black men selling other blacks into slavery. As Schuyler notes in the Foreword:

In Liberia . . . modern servitude is strikingly ironic because this black republic was founded by freed Negro slaves from the United States a century ago as a haven for all oppressed black people. Its proud motto reads, "The Love of Liberty Brought Us Here," but the aborigines find little liberty under the Negro masters (v).

Nor did Schuyler ignore the white man's role. Noting in the Foreword that slavery existed in America under whites and that it still exists in Africa, the East Indies, and the South Seas ("in the colonies of European powers"), Schuyler says:

If this novel can help arouse enlightened world opinion against this brutalizing of the native population in a Negro republic, perhaps the conscience of civilized people will stop similar atrocities in native lands ruled by proud white nations that boast of their superior culture (vi).

There are hints throughout the novel that Schuyler perceived yet another irony. The most brutal Americo-Liberians have all been educated in American or European schools, or at least spent some time in white society, and have thus adopted the mentality and excesses of whites. (African leaders who have been Europeanized and "whitened" are sometimes referred to as "black whitemen."[14]) A few examples must suffice.

Sidney Cooper Johnson, the president of Liberia, is the descendant of "pioneer grandparents" who carved a nation out of the wilderness, yet "educated in the United States and trained in the law, he preferred a life of ease, political intrigue and polite conversation to the worries and rigors of tropical agriculture" (11). David Jackson, though not nearly so well-educated, represented the Liberian government "as a consul in England," where he learned to love the good life. Like the finest British lord, he insists on being carried from village to village in the bush, he drinks only Scotch, he has a refrigerator, and he insists on a morning tub, five o'clock tea, and formal dress at dinner! His wife, a bored and bitchy pseudoaristocrat who takes great delight in beating the heroine whenever possible, earned a Bachelor of Arts degree "from an American Negro college in the United States" (227). Even Sammy Williams acquired an education in the United States: "Much of [his] versatility was due to a considerable sojourn in the United States, whence he had been sent by his parents many years ago to attend one of the larger universities" (136–37). While in the states, he forged a check, was caught, and was sent to Sing Sing "where he learned much from his

associates that was useful when he entered Liberian politics. . ."
(137).

Saunders and even Henderson, the two "good" Americo-
Liberians, were also educated in the states, but they do not practice
the vices or absurd mannerisms of their villainous counterparts.
Schuyler seems to be saying that a "white" education is not inher-
ently corrupting so long as foreign students carefully avoid the
vices and foibles of the host country (Schuyler approved of close ties
between the United States and Liberia, so long as the "progressive
elements" in both societies worked together; this view is set forth in
later articles such as "Uncle Sam's Black Step-Child"). But once a
Liberian begins to behave like the very worst white colonizer or
slaver, then he can no longer serve his country.

If the villains in *Slaves Today* are somewhat like those in *Black No
More*, then the heroes are representative of the Schuylerian virtues
of decency, self-sufficiency, tolerance, love, and good will. Time
and time again Schuyler intimates that native life is the ideal life,
that it is filled with dignity, courage, and a sense of tradition. The
"true African" is contrasted with the evil and filth of Monrovia, from
the time we encounter the "dignified native chiefs" (10) awaiting an
audience with the president until the end of the book. Describing
the wedding of Zo and Pameta, Schuyler waxes poetic about the
beauty of native African dance:

Africa loves to dance. Almost every night when the tropical moon illumines
village streets as if they were lighted by arc lights, the variously pitched
drums tap out their intricate rhythm and the close-packed crowd shuffles,
leaps and hops to exhaustion.

Few forms of entertainment prove superior to the African dance in all its
variations. The roll-tap-and-boom of the drum sends peculiar tingles over
the body. The inhibitions of industrial society drop gradually from even the
most civilized person until he also wants to join the gyrating, stamping black
folk. The dance, the drums, the horns—these musical instruments are ages
old. They have come down from the dawn of humanity. They are a part of
our heritage. No wonder all humans are drawn to them (32–33).

Similarly, Schuyler reveals both knowledge of and appreciation for
African tradition in his descriptions of the wedding (23ff), the native
doctor (27ff), the praise singers who celebrate the oral history of the
African community (35–37), and the integration of all life rhythms
with the supernatural (35). Especially interesting for someone who
has spent time in West Africa is Schuyler's perception of the dignity

and awe accorded a tribal chief—"the father of his village"—to whom "the . . . folk defer and pay homage" and "whose word is law." "Parents point to him as an example their children should follow if they would also become great. That he should be humiliated by a public whipping before his people is unthinkable to them" (49).

Aside from stressing the tradition and dignity of ancient Africa, Schuyler also attempts to explain the greatness of pre-colonial Africa. Writing in an era when Africa was still considered the "dark continent" inhabited by savages, Schuyler was far ahead of his time in glorifying an ancient village which was "once the stronghold of a great and warlike king, the tread of whose armies shook the ground" (108).

Schuyler, though obviously charmed by Africa, was intent in *Slaves Today* on linking the African native with men the world over. One of his major themes is the universal humanity of mankind (Schuyler told me in 1975 that he was always an avowed internationalist). Although African customs may seem exotic and her music and lifestyles may be different from Western music and lifestyles, yet her people are at one with people the world over. The most "unsophisticated" native, Schuyler says, "thinks and feels like most human beings the world over" (79). Actually, Schuyler's real purpose is to universalize the Liberia story, pitting humanists wherever they reside against the sadists and evildoers who manipulate them. In one passage in particular Schuyler puts this concept into focus. Speaking of Jackson and Captain Burns, he says:

The two officials were but slightly less dark than the natives over whom they ruled but they felt no kinship with [them] for that reason. It was no more difficult for them to oppress and exploit fellow black men than it usually is for powerful whites to do the same thing to fellow white men. Color did not enter here—it was class that counted (100).

Class—or caste (as in *Black No More* and in many of Schuyler's articles)—is the true evil in the world.

The ideal Liberian in *Slaves Today* is not the bush native. No matter how many humane qualities he possesses or how good a man he is, he is no match for the evil forces that rule in Monrovia. The person in the novel who represents the ideal merging of African and Western values, the only man who is truly prepared to bring together the best of both worlds, is Tom Saunders. Education, talent, inclination, and foresight have prepared Saunders for this role: "A naturalized citizen hailing originally from America and filled with Yankee ideas of business and efficiency," Saunders stands almost alone among Liberian leaders, fighting "hard against the destructive, reactionary forces in the little republic" and believing "that the policies and practices of the ruling class would eventually end in the ruination of Liberia" (140). The man who introduced effective industrial concepts to Liberia and founded the opposition party inevitably attracted "a devoted and loyal group of the younger Liberians . . . who are eager to put a stop to the evils that were undermining and destroying the state" (141). Even though Saunders loses the election at the end of the novel, he will continue to fight the good fight, "to lay his life on the line" (141) to restore Liberia to her true position as a great black republic.

Schuyler's major themes in *Slaves Today,* then, are not much different from those in *Black No More,* except that by the time he finished his Liberian adventure, Schuyler had become an "internationalist" who believed that the problems facing the United States were not unique. He developed a philosophy which might seem a cliché—namely, that men of evil intent and men of good will exist side by side in every society in the world. Schuyler insisted in *Slaves Today* that the common man possesses the same qualities and fights the same battles that men the world over must fight.

V *The Critical Response*

Some critics, as noted earlier, took offense almost immediately to Schuyler's Liberia articles and presumably aggravated their anger further by reading the book. But a number of critics had favorable things to say about the novel. H. L. Mencken said in *The American Mercury* that Schuyler "is rather too indignant to be altogether convincing" and that *Slaves Today* suggests "the manner of *Uncle Tom's Cabin.*" Yet there are "some excellent pictures of native life in it, and the native characters, in the main, are better done than the 'civilized' Liberians." Mencken also noted that Schuyler's book was "based on first-hand observation."[15] *The New York Evening Post* praised the book, saying that Schuyler "has become one of the most effective of the Negro publicists" and "has outgrown an assumption of the Mencken attack," that he has proved once again that "he can arrest specific quackeries, pomps, and cruelties . . . with a blunt truculence, a vigilant and scornful penetration" that indicates an irony which "has long been a richly vernacular scythe."

The same reviewer says that he had expected a novel in which "the correction of abuses" would be "more important than character":

> On the contrary, Mr. Schuyler has revealed a new gift in telling a quick, ferocious and authentically moving story in terms at once particular to his creations and typical of that pitiless milieu they move in, a story which degenerates into sketchy melodrama only at its close. Even so, his ending is true to circumstances and people, rightly felt and formally satisfactory, deficient only in some haste or indignant baldness in its realization.[16]

The reviewer touches on a few more points, then makes this assessment: "Mr. Schuyler's interest in satire is beginning to be engaged not merely by conflict between races or within a race, but by the more largely human . . ."[17]

Dewey R. Jones, writing in *Opportunity*, presents the black perspective. He believes that *Slaves Today* is "a definite improvement" over *Black No More* because the novel "is told in a far more effective manner." Written with zest, *Slaves Today* reveals for all black America the manner in which the Americo-Liberians exploit Liberian natives; Schuyler's facts only "add to the disgust with which most Afro-Americans consider Liberia and her political condition"—a comment that probably more accurately reflects the black mood of the day than did the comments of the Garveyites. The heart of Jones' review occurs in this passage:

> There are many people who believe that fiction is a greater crusading agency against social evils than are weighty factual tomes. They cite *Uncle Tom's Cabin* as a fine example of the truth of their position. Perhaps Mr. Schuyler is of this school and had a very definite message to give to the world. . . . If he is and had, he has succeeded admirably, for the book certainly reeks with the stuff from which indignation is made. Even Negroes who have been wont to consider Liberia from a distant and disinterested point of view must alter their opinions and think a little more soberly about this African Republic after reading this book.[18]

Mary W. Ovington, the grande dame of the NAACP, noted the effect *Slaves Today* should have on black America. It "is stark tragedy," a novel that "should make every American Negro who reads it cease to talk of the brutal white man," for "brutality does not depend on race but upon opportunity." If a man is given the power "to exploit his fellow man," she continues, "he will take advantage of it." It is America's mandate, she concludes, to study what is happening in Liberia, to censure its barbarism, and to do "everything possible to strengthen that humane minority of which Schuyler writes."[19]

Even the *New York Times* critic praised *Slaves Today* for its social significance. The novel

is absorbingly interesting both as fiction and as an exposé of conditions recalling the horrors of the Belgian Congo. Where a less objective author dealing with an exotic theme would lapse into sentimentality and high-flown descriptive writing, Mr. Schuyler has avoided these pitfalls. There is plenty of action and pithy dialogue. The rotund, smiling hypocrite who is Vice President and the crafty cynic in the Presidential chair are vividly and convincingly portrayed.[20]

Whereas Robert Bone and others tend to ignore *Slaves Today*, Arthur P. Davis has made pertinent comments on its strengths and weaknesses. Schuyler, notes Davis, reveals again that he has "a journalist's mind, a satirist's mind" and so his characters are manipulated and one-dimensional. His love story, Davis continues, "simply [does] not move us." "Read today as a work of art," he concludes, "*Slaves Today* is disappointing."[21]

I cannot help but agree with Professor Davis on his major point—namely, that *Slaves Today* is not great fiction—though I do feel that the Fernando Po scenes and some of the jungle scenes are quite good. *Slaves Today* is much better propaganda than art. More important, it is *journalistic* fiction and should be judged by journalistic rather than other standards. Finally, it is historically significant because it is the first attempt at a realistic assessment of Africa by a black writer.

I think Schuyler realized his novel's strengths and weaknesses. The novel, he told me during the interview, was written in two or three months: "I was still recovering from malaria, and I was trying to do a million things all at once." Yet "there's a lot of good stuff in it too. My descriptions were based on those [people] I met and interviewed."[22]

Schuyler did not intend to produce the great American novel in *Slaves Today.* He intended to write an incisive and sensationalist novel that would move people to action. That he wrote a muckraking novel in the grand old manner is without question. That it did not reform the world is unfortunate.

CHAPTER 7

The Later Years: Black and Conservative

F OR the historian few books contain as much information on black
America in the twentieth century as Schuyler's *Black and Conservative.* The most attractive aspect of this autobiography is the
loving compilation of anecdotes, letters, columns, and reminiscences by a man who knew every major black figure from the 1920s
on. I have seen black scholars settle a dispute over a name, a place,
or an event by referring to *Black and Conservative.* The "black" part
of *Black and Conservative* is a treasure trove.

The "conservative" part of *Black and Conservative* is what upsets
many a critic and scholar. The second half of Schuyler's book,
though it continues to provide illuminating background material
(much of which has been used in this study, both in footnotes and in
the text), contains Schuyler's exposé of Communists, "red Uncle
Toms" who have knowingly participated or been duped, and black
"agitators" who have inflamed the race issue. This is the part of the
autobiography that earned Schuyler a reputation for being a reactionary, a black man aiding and abetting the white establishment, a
fanatic who marched to "the sounds of a different drummer."[1]

That *Black and Conservative* is good autobiography is without
question. Schuyler's easy style, his anecdotes and character
sketches, his organization from beginning to end, reveal a man at
the height of his writing ability. The book could serve as an excellent
model for freshman composition students, journalists, and researchers.

The only stylistic problem is the way that Schuyler unsuccessfully
mixes anecdotes and propaganda. One begins to feel that Schuyler
was asked to write an autobiography celebrating the values of
conservatism and that he agreed only on the condition that he might
include his own memoirs. Frequently Schuyler jerks back from a

delightful anecdote when he remembers he is supposed to be writing conservatively; then the polemics begin—and continue. Was his first intention to write a highly readable autobiography or a conservative manifesto? We do not find the answer in *Black and Conservative.*

I *Part One: Chapters One–Eleven*

The best way to approach Schuyler's autobiography is to consider it as two distinct works. In the first part, the reader encounters by now familiar characters and incidents: Schuyler's mother and grandmother; army acquaintances; the lean years in the Bowery; the first years at *The Messenger* and *The Pittsburgh Courier;* his development as a satirist, journalist, lecturer; his Southern tour in 1925–1926; his Liberian investigation. The Seattle bar incident related in Chapter 1 demonstrates Schuyler's anecdotal ability. Here's another one, about wide open San Francisco as seen through the eyes of a young army private around 1913:

Two flights down in the cellar of one [gambling] place was allegedly the biggest game of craps in the district, and it had the dubious distinction of being run by a tall, cream-colored, pleasingly plump colored woman with full red lips and a mouth full of gold teeth. This was Gold Tooth Mame who could cut a craps game with the best of them. Wearing a John B. Stetson hat and a box back coat that only touched her on the shoulders, she presided over the game like a veteran, calling the dice in a deep voice.

"Th' ma-an th'owed eight! Eighty-eight, eighty-eight! Take yo' money tuh Sistuh Kate! Brutha, yoh point is eight! Let th' dice roll, gaddam you soul!"

To reinforce her decisions, Mame had a .45 revolver parked near her right hand, but nobody disputed her. The room was crammed with as nondescript a crowd of ruffians as one could assemble. . . . When a player threw craps, she would bellow, "Shoot, nigger! You ain't los' nuthin' but yoh money!"

Not even "Rough House" Reed, a wiry, black fellow out of the slums of Chicago who was acknowledged to be the roughest man in [our] battalion, was able to faze her. When he familiarly put his hand on her shoulder, she turned in a flash and snarled, "You gittin' ready tuh shave with one han' foh th' rest o' yoh life!"[2]

Schuyler always had a genuine fondness for and good rapport with the colorful citizens of the underworld. It is to these people that he turned again and again, no matter what city or country he was investigating, for the truth.

He also discusses most of the Harlem intellectuals of the 1920s. As Arthur P. Davis has noted, one of the values of *Black and Conservative* is that Schuyler knew every important figure during the Harlem Renaissance, yet he owed allegiance to no one camp. His objectivity, Davis suggests, is what makes his memoirs invaluable.[3] Schuyler provides us with fascinating details about Marcus Garvey and the "Back-to-Africa" movement, about Du Bois, about authors major and minor, about the journalists, teachers, and politicians that debated the issues of the day; yet always he seems most impressed with the person who laughs at life (e.g., his mother, some fellow officers, and various employers practiced "a healthy cynicism") and is self-made, independent, reliable, tough. An early model was A. Philip Randolph, "one of the finest, most engaging men I had ever met":

Slender, brown-skinned, handsome, erect and always immaculately dressed, he was undemanding and easy to get along with. He was leisurely and undisturbed, remaining affable under all circumstances, whether the rent was due [for *The Messenger* office] and he did not have it, or whether an expected donation failed to materialize, or whether the long-suffering printer in Brooklyn was demanding money. He had a keen sense of humor and laughed easily, even in adversity. . . . His aplomb seemed impenetrable. With the sonorous voice and the delivery of a Shakespearian actor, he calmed all tension, anger, and insistent creditors (135–36).

Schuyler could even admire a Communist if he had a sense of humor. In the 1920s Benjamin Davis, Jr., "was not a Communist, was not even thinking about it, but even after he became one we always got on well together." "He was," notes Schuyler, "one of the few Communists I knew who had a sense of humor. . . . Then, too, Ben had a considerable streak of . . . cynicism" (167).

II   *Part Two: Chapters Twelve–Nineteen*

At what point Schuyler became the foe of Communism is hard to determine. He says in his autobiography that he had grown cynical about the movement as early as 1922 and that he joined the fray in earnest in 1932 because of the Communist's behavior during the Scottsboro trial. He would like us believe that he was a conservative from the beginning and joined the Socialist Party merely to find out what the opposition was up to. But as readers of *The Pittsburgh Courier* have told me, Schuyler's "Views and Reviews" columns did not become truly reactionary until the 1950s during the McCarthy era. And it was not until he was an old man attacking Martin Luther King that *The Pittsburgh Courier* began to refuse to publish his columns. Comparing his Columbia Oral History interview (1960) with *Black and Conservative* reveals that in six years, Schuyler had become much more adamant about Communism. I suspect that one purpose of *Black and Conservative* is to make his conversion to anti-Communism seem to occur earlier than in fact it did.

If we can believe what Schuyler says in *Black and Conservative*, the basis for his conservatism was rooted in his childhood. He was born in the North, was reared in fairly comfortable middle class surroundings, and received an early education in the New England virtues of thrift, self-confidence, independence, and industry. Such a man would take pride in making it on his own, in learning how to cope—gracefully yet cynically—without self-pity. Thus, Schuyler's prefatory comments in *Black and Conservative* are not at all inconsistent with what we have already learned about the man: "The lifetime endeavor of the intelligent Negro is how to be reasonably happy though colored":

Contrary to the pundits on the Negro (or Caucasian!) problem who bewail the American racial facts of life, most of the colored brethren do not go about perpetually enveloped in gloom and despair. . . . Of course, not being insane, they are not always happy and gay, as traditional "Southrons" have insisted for a century. . . .

The American Negro is a prime example of the survival of the fittest, and it is enlightening to contrast his position today with that of the Amerindian. He has been the outstanding example of American conservatism: adjustable, resourceful, adaptable, patient, restrained, and not given to gambling what advantages he has in quixotic adventures. . . . Through the succeeding uproars and upheavals that have attended our national development, the Negro has adjusted himself to every change with the basic aim of survival and advancement. *Had he taken the advice of the minority of firebrands in his midst, he would have been exterminated* (1–2; my italics).

It is black America's ability to adapt, to survive in the face of possible extermination, that Schuyler most admires:

The ability to conserve, consolidate, and change when expedient is the hallmark of individual and group intelligence. It is why the Negro will always be here. As the law, history, and literature show, no other element of the population has had a more profound effect on our national life. They have less reason than any others to harbor any feelings of inferiority, although naturally they suffer from frustration (2).

This is a theme that Schuyler returned to again and again in his early writing: only the black inferiority complex (which leads to the "urge to whiteness" manifested in the use of skin lighteners and hair straighteners) can undermine the staying power, the stubbornness that has characterized the Afro-American. The doctrine, of course, is double-edged: a healthy superiority complex leads to the self-confidence needed to cut a path through life regardless of the odds; but it also can lead to a "pragmatism" grounded in expediency—an attitude that might please many who oppose immediate racial reform.

Recognizing Schuyler's philosophy of expediency, it becomes fairly obvious why he attacked Communism. As many Negro intellectuals have realized, the Communists did attempt to seduce the black leadership of this country with "solutions" such as the separatist concept of a "black belt" stretching across the South. Schuyler felt that the Communists were using black frustrations to create chaos in the United States, that they encouraged (and sensationalized) riots, lynchings, and other racial troubles in order to polarize black and white America. He sensed early that Communist claims of "brotherhood" with black America were hypocritical, that blacks were merely pawns in the grand design. Consequently, he believed that Negroes might well be committing suicide by putting in with the Communists. Interestingly enough, black spokesmen as disparate as Langston Hughes, Claude McKay, and Ralph Ellison, all of whom flirted with Communism, realized eventually that the party's design was anathema to black progress. It is a reality that Ralph Ellison described brilliantly in *Invisible Man*. [4]

Realizing the strategy of the Communists, Schuyler determined to devote his efforts to fighting them and those "red Uncle Toms" who furthered their cause (190): "It was abundantly clear to me that I must devote all of my energies to fighting this conspiracy to destroy the Negro population to ensure a Communist victory. I had one potent weapon—my typewriter" (191).

Tied in with this is Schuyler's attitude toward almost every civil rights leader who "agitated" the race situation. Marcus Garvey invited racial genocide by urging physical separation. From Schuyler's point of view, Martin Luther King or Malcolm X or the Black Muslims were just as dangerous, because their various programs invited racial polarization, a breakdown in interracial communications, and eventual destruction. Black America must avoid the punishment that the American Indian endured when he was forced to accept second class citizenship and to live on reservations. This is not to excuse Schuyler's more preposterous statements:

From the beginning of the so-called Negro Revolution and the insane antics identified with it, I had taken the same position editorially and in my column that I had throughout the years. I had opposed all the Marches on Washington and other mob demonstrations, recognizing them as part of the Red techniques of agitation, infiltration, and subversion (341).

The Issue [of racial conflict] is much too serious to permit a handful of dreamers and self-serving schemers to divide the country further, increase irritation, resentment and hatred, and thus hasten the likelihood of civil strife, which has been the goal of the international Communist conspiracy for more than forty years (351).

[I fought for] Senator Joseph R. McCarthy, a well-intentioned politician who was appalled by what he learned of the wide ramifications of the Communist conspiracy. . . . [He] was . . . a great American (330).

Neither directly nor indirectly has Dr. King made any contribution to world (or even domestic) peace. Methinks the Lenin Prize would have been more appropriate [than the Nobel Prize for Peace], since it is no mean feat for one so young to acquire 60 Communist front citations. . . . Dr. King's principal contribution to world peace has been to roam the country like some sable Typhoid Mary, infecting the mentally disturbed with perversion of Christian doctrine, and grabbing fat lecture fees from the shallow-pated.[5]

It is not hard to imagine the ultimate fate of a society in which a pixilated criminal like Malcolm X is almost universally praised, and has hospitals, schools, and highways named in his memory! . . . We might as well call out the school children to celebrate the birthday of Benedict Arnold. Or to raise a monument to Alger Hiss. We would do well to remember that all societies are destroyed from within—through weakness, immorality, crime, debauchery, and failing mentality.[6]

Yet outlandish as his comments seem, it should be noted that Schuyler always had the survival of the black race uppermost in his thoughts. He realized clearly that the major problem of the twentieth century is the color line; he also believed that black America would lose everything if it came to a final confrontation, a confrontation which he saw being brought about by racial "agitators." Like other black leaders, he pinpointed the problem; however, he could not accept any of the moderate solutions that have been proposed. The passages cited above might well comfort those whites dedicated to gradualism. But Schuyler's final words in *Black and Conservative* do not provide them much comfort. The marches, riots, and demonstrations, he says, "were proposed, incited, managed, and led by professional agitators, whose only interest in the workers was to exploit them":

Under the influence of their white (or Red) mentors, a contaminated Negro leadership snapped at the Communist bait, received *the support of white "liberals" charting a course of disaster,* and like the pied pipers led the lunatic fringe astray. . . . I held to my position. Of course this made me an "Uncle Tom" to those people who had no answers to what I was writing and saying (342; my italics).

Not having any illusions about white people *per se,* I have long been fearful that this increasing racial animosity . . . might lead to actual civil war which would certainly lead to genocide. Nobody who knows history can discount this. . . . whites also have their callous and craven politicians, their professional agitators, and their swarms of the mentally deficient, . . . I have not forgotten that an American administration put more than 100,000 Japanese Americans in concentration camps only twenty-four years ago. . . . Nor is the fate of the Amerindians . . . to be forgotten (344–45).

Not a few black (and white) militants have said the same things. Another point that Schuyler stresses is even more significant. It is one I have heard made time and time again—namely, that there is too much emphasis (especially by white liberals) on failure in the black community. Says Schuyler:

radical Negro agitators . . . have been engaging in a veritable campaign of Negro mass disparagement. They write theses on the "failure" of the Negro family, dwell on the "helplessness" of the colored community, emphasize the high incidence of crime, disease, narcotics addiction, and other social evils. The white sociologists and welfarists vie with them with a suspicious relish *reminiscent of the Negrophobic propaganda of a half century before, when such hatemongers as Thomas Dixon held sway.* The picture . . . that emerges is pessimistic and frightening, tending to make insistence on integration ridiculous. Thus, the proclaimed aims are defeated in advance. . . . Racial adjustment is delicate and difficult enough without the efforts of all the sorcerer's apprentices who for the past half decade have devoted themselves to performing miracles that became shambles (351; my italics).

At the end of *Black and Conservative,* Schuyler forecasts a somewhat idealized future—a dream, perhaps, but one that should be considered:

In our future America we need to stress the importance of the individual of whatever color. . . . There will be no color war here if we work not to have one, although some kind of color line there may always be, as there is elsewhere in the world. We do not need to share the wealth as much as we need to share our heritage so that all may proudly claim ownership in it. We need to strive to become one people in our resolution, determination, and achievement instead of two people, colored and white (352).

These quotations show that Schuyler continued through his life to emphasize many of the same themes he had been stressing since the 1920s. The major problem of the twentieth century, he insists, is the color line. Whites are in the majority. Though racism is obviously atrocious, improvements are occurring.

To avoid agitation of the race issue and consequent radical extinction, it is necessary for enlightened men of both races to work together for a better tomorrow. Racial intermarriage is one solution, but not a likely one in a country filled with distrust of such marriages. Legislation may accomplish some of the goals of black America. But the real breakthroughs will be caused by men of confidence, ability, courage, independence, and resourcefulness. Feelings of inferiority are self-defeating, as are the influences of outside forces, such as Communism, that exploit America's "color-phobia." Once black America realizes this, it can move toward total manhood rights.

CHAPTER 8

Schuyler as Satirist and Journalistic Iconoclast

SCHUYLER has contributed much in several areas. "The Negro-Art Hokum" is probably the most articulate definition of one theory of the role of black authors in a white society; the issues it raises have not yet been laid to rest. "Black Art" and the other *American Mercury* pieces are among the best that appeared in that publication during the 1920s and 1930s. Series like "Aframerica Today" and "Slavery in Liberia" are significant contributions to the history of investigative reporting.

But Schuyler will be remembered mainly for his satire and for his role as gadfly. As one of the major authors of the Harlem Renaissance, he wrote a satire that became a prototype. And as part of that "peculiarly American" group of journalistic iconoclasts, Schuyler took his place in a literary tradition represented by Ambrose Bierce and William Cowper Brann in the nineteenth century and by H. L. Mencken and the black journalists of the early twentieth century. Though satire and iconoclastic literature are often indistinguishable, they will be considered here as separate types.

I Schuyler as Black Satirist

Harlem Renaissance critics knew instinctively that the author of essays like "Blessed Are The Sons of Ham," "Our Greatest Gift to America," and *Black No More* was making a unique contribution to black American letters. Schuyler, they realized, was the first writer to attack "the major problem of the twentieth century"[1] (in Du Bois' phrase) with the weapon of ridicule. No black writer before Schuyler underscored the fundamental absurdities of America's "colorphobia" with such devastating wit and scorn.

When Alain Locke said that in *Black No More* "one of the great veins of Negro fiction has been opened,"[2] he was expressing the majority view. He would have been in total agreement with Hugh Gloster, who said in 1948 that "American Negroes have usually handled racial issues with painful seriousness and, in calling attention to social abuses, have almost invariably failed to appropriate the value of rollicking satire as a vehicle for the exposure of injustice and hypocrisy."[3] Schuyler not only recognized the potential in satire, he exploited it with imagination. In doing so, he broke with the past and set a pattern for the future.

This is not to say that black writers had never before used satire. The absurdity of disfranchisement and second class citizenship in a democracy has always been a fit subject for irony. Writers like Martin Delany, Sutton Griggs, Charles W. Chesnutt, James Weldon Johnson, W.E.B. Du Bois, Rudolph Fisher, and Wallace Thurman produced short stories or novels prior to 1931 that contained elements of satire. But none of these authors produced a full length satire like *Black No More*.

Black No More, however, is more than just another "first." It is also without doubt "the best work of prose satire to come from the New Negro Movement,"[4] even including Thurman's *Infants of the Spring*. Whereas Thurman's target was the Harlem Renaissance itself, Schuyler's province was no less than all of America, North and South; past, present, and future; black and white. Thurman's Juvenalian attack occasionally falters; Schuyler's is consistent.

Indeed, scholars may someday recognize that *Black No More* is the prototype for twentieth century black satire, from Thurman's book and Langston Hughes' *The Ways of White Folks* and the Jesse B. Semple ("Simple") tales, through Ralph Ellison's *Invisible Man*, William Melvin Kelley's *A Different Drummer*, Hal Bennett's *A Wilderness of Vines*, *The Black Wine*, and *The Lord of Dark Places*, Harry Beckham's *Runner Mack*, to Ishmael Reed's *The Free-Lance Pallbearers*, *Yellow Back Radio Broke Down*, *Mumbo Jumbo*, and *The Last Days of Louisiana Red*. Schuyler's sustained attack anticipates Thurman's and Bennett's. His *picaro* hero appears and reappears in different guises in Hughes, Ellison, Kelley, and Reed. Schuyler's Horatian lightheartedness (in the early pages of *Black No More*) anticipates Hughes' tone, and his Juvenalian wrath (in the final chapters of *Black No More*) anticipates the invective of Thurman, Bennett, and Kelley. His Rabelasian bawdiness anticipates Ishmael Reed. Schuyler's attack on black institutions and leaders, like his equally vehement attack on white bigotry and violence, anticipates just about every major satirist in the twentieth century. (Double-edged satire, indeed, is the hallmark not only of black writers but of the famous black stand-up artists, from the late Moms Mabley and Redd Foxx to Dick Gregory and Richard Pryor. Slapping both blacks and whites is not unique with Schuyler; it is characteristic of black satire everywhere.) Finally, the scope and narrative structure that Schuyler employs have been repeated in the work of Ellison, Bennett, and Reed. Whether or not these and other modern satirists owe a direct debt to Schuyler, they did inherit, shape, and enrich the materials he worked with in 1931.

A few critics have even commented on the obvious relevancy of *Black No More*. Arthur P. Davis, perhaps reacting to the black consciousness movement of the 1960s and early 1970s, argues that Schuyler's novel "should appeal to today's readers almost as much as it did to the 1931 audience." He continues: "Although most Negroes have no desire to be white, many of them have become just as foolish about *blackness* as their parents and grandparents were about *whiteness* in 1931. Human nature has a depressing habit of remaining the same" (italics in original).[5] Hugh Gloster stresses the universality of *Black No More* in these words: "It lays bare the pusillanimity, stupidity, selfishness, opportunism, and materialism of Americans, white as well as black." It demonstrates that "adultery, graft, and debauchery are . . . failings of men of high position in both races." The implication of *Black No More*, then, is that "human beings . . . are fundamentally the same under the skin."[6] Schuyler's attack on our "colorphobia" has universal appeal because it is based on ancient satiric assumptions: we are all living in "this insane asylum," and we can always count on man's inhumanity to his fellow man.

II *Schuyler as Journalistic Iconoclast*

Schuyler's harsh iconoclasm, says Davis, "slashes . . . at all American . . . color shibboleths. . . ."[7] Schuyler "made fun of everything," A. Philip Randolph is quoted as saying.[8] Schuyler, admonished an editorial in *The Crisis* (1965), is "a veteran dissenter and incurable iconoclast" who "dips his pen in his ever-handy bottle of acid." He "has been . . . busy breaking idols. . . ."[9] Iconoclasm is a word that has been used often to describe George Schuyler. From 1923 on, Schuyler was one of that select breed of moral crusaders and apparent social misfits who, as journalists, delighted in breaking the idols of the tribe. They attacked, often ferociously and personally, big businessmen, government officials, and other "exploiters" of the average American. Like satirists, they hoped to reform, though one wonders if they would really have been happy if society suddenly became rational.

Ambrose Bierce, the "caustic columnist" from San Francisco, was attacked on the streets (as well as sued for libel in a case that was laughed out of court) for his "Town Crier" columns, in which he mocked specific causes, specific people. Before he disappeared over the border into Mexico in 1913, Bierce compiled *The Devil's Dictionary* and *The Satanic Reader*. An iconoclast, he said in his *Dictionary*, "is a breaker of idols, the worshipers whereof are imperfectly gratified by the performance, and most strenuously protest that he unbuildeth but doth not re-edify, that he pulleth down but pileth not up."[10]

"Brann the Iconoclast," Bierce's contemporary, attacked public idols so viciously that he was eventually forced to establish his own publication—*Brann's Iconoclast*—which he produced in Waco, Texas from 1895 until his death in 1898. "The iconoclast," he wrote in a typical diatribe against a Baptist preacher who had accused him of atheism, has the mission to "expose Frauds and abolish Fakes, to make unrelenting war upon Humbugs and Hypocrites."[11] Brann made war until he was shot by a disgruntled reader (though "he had the courage, with strength enough, to turn and fatally wound his antagonist" before he died). His humor was "a whip" with which he "scourged from the temples of social purity every intruder there."[12]

Sixteen years after Brann was shot, and one year after Bierce disappeared, the "iconoclast from Baltimore" became co-editor of *The Smart Set*. In 1924 he founded and edited *The American Mercury*, perhaps the most influential (if irreverent) of the 1920s and 1930s journals. "Iconoclasm" said Mencken, is effective if "at least one visitor to the shrine is left full of doubts." The "liberation of the human mind has been furthered by gay fellows who heaved dead cats into sanctuaries."[13] By 1933, when he felt the Roosevelt administration had betrayed its promise, Mencken found that he was "breasting currents too strong for him." Nevertheless he was *the* great iconoclast of this century—and friend and mentor to Schuyler, as we have already seen.

Schuyler had much in common with these men. Like Bierce's "Town Crier," Schuyler's "Shafts and Darts" and "Views and Reviews" attacked specific fools in short, pithy paragraphs. Schuyler's "galloping Juvenalian invective" was much like Brann's "whip" that scourged and excoriated. And his mature satire—"Our Greatest Gift to America," for example—is much like the longer pieces Mencken wrote in his best days. All four, interestingly, became more conservative the older they got. All four suffered either physically or socially for their efforts to shape society. All four despaired of ridding the world of its "Frauds . . . and Fakes, . . . Humbugs and Hypocrites."[14]

Though of the same school as Mencken and the others, Schuyler was spiritually allied in tone, theme, and style with fellow black iconoclasts during the 1920s. He was discovered and tutored by Chandler Owen and A. Philip Randolph. He worked side by side with Theophilus Lewis and Wallace Thurman at *The Messenger* (Lewis collaborated with him on "Shafts and Darts" for a year). With DuBois he attacked the Ku Klux Klan, lynchings, do-nothing politicians, and misguided race leaders.

But of this group, Schuyler was the one who became the truest iconoclast, blending just the right amounts of ridicule and reform and sustaining the "gadfly" tone column after column, week after week. Owen, Randolph, Lewis, and Du Bois rarely produced the slashing humor that Schuyler did. Thurman came closest to matching Schuyler's style, but he did not have the national audience that Schuyler had, nor did he live long enough to develop to his full potential.

It soon becomes apparent why Schuyler had to spend his life marching to "the sounds of a different drummer."[15] In his quest to expose sham and hypocrisy, Schuyler was frequently censured for his bluntness or savagery. Like most satirists and iconoclasts, Schuyler was never in any danger of becoming one of the top ten favorites. No writer who attacks the idols of the tribe wins popularity contests.

Moreover, Schuyler was often censured for turning from writing about issues to attempting action. He was a reformer. He was not satisfied to write about Africa (or Latin America, or Europe, or the South) from his armchair. He had to go to Liberia, experience hardships and danger, explore the issues, and then write his articles. Of course, instead of reforming Liberia (let alone the rest of the world), Schuyler merely incurred first the hostility and then the indifference of his readers. Similarly, he turned from writing about cooperative efforts to establishing a Young Negroes' Cooperative

League, for he sincerely believed that cooperatives would make Afro-Americans as self-sufficient as he himself was. His league failed. Still later, Schuyler became tired of just talking about the dangers of Marxism and entered a political race against the formidable Adam Clayton Powell. He lost the campaign.

As more information about Schuyler's life surfaces, a pattern does begin to emerge: whenever he stopped writing about an issue and set about trying to take action, he met defeat. Again and again this happened and the young idealist inevitably grew older and more disillusioned with each failure. Perhaps his failure to change life led to his increasingly pessimistic, reactionary, and "out of step" posture.

It is a shame, in a way, that Schuyler could not have resigned himself to his own satiric vision of man, namely, that we are all the inhabitants of an insane asylum. The history of literature is crowded with satirists who never really accepted the implications of their own message. Schuyler, like so many others, preached that the world was crazy but believed (secretly, of course) that it was reformable. And therein lies the true path to lonely iconoclasm.

Notes and References

Preface

1. See Robert Bone, *The Negro Novel in America* (New Haven, 1965), pp. 5–8 and 89–94, for definitions of "assimilationist" and "the urge to whiteness"; and Charles R. Larson's "Introduction" to *Black No More* (New York, 1971) for the comment that "the sounds of a different drummer are clearly what George S. Schuyler has marched to down through the years" (p. 13). Also see below, Chapter 5, on the critical reception of *Black No More*. "Assimilationism" means to be absorbed into the cultural tradition of a (larger) population or group and best corresponds to the word "integration" when we speak of black Americans in relation to white America. In both Bone and Larson, however, the term "assimilation" has other, more negative connotations: to be an "assimilationist," a black writer has to be willing to "sell out" or deny his black heritage. An "Uncle Tom" is a person who practices such racial disloyalty.

2. W. E. B. Du Bois, "The Browsing Reader," *The Crisis*, 39 (March 1931), 100; Arthur P. Davis, *From the Dark Tower* (Washington, 1974), pp. 104–108; and comments by Henry Lee Moon and Rayford Logan in Hollie I. West's "A Black, Biting John Bircher," *The Washington Post*, September 6, 1973, p. C-1.

Chapter One

1. *Black and Conservative* (New Rochelle, 1971), p. 223. Further references will be given in the text.

2. I interviewed Schuyler on October 1, 1973, October 6, 1973, and May 14, 1975. Additional material was acquired in interviews and correspondence with William Loeb, Arthur P. Davis, Woodrow Taylor, Eugene Grigsby, and Charles Larson. A significant interview was conducted by Ishmael Reed and Steve Cannon in 1972; it was published in *Shrovetide in Old New Orleans* (New York, 1978), pp. 195–218.

3. George Goodman, Jr., "George Schuyler, Black Author," *The New York Times*, September 8, 1977, p. 40.

4. "The Reminiscences of George S. Schuyler" (New York, 1960), p. 7. Hereafter, "Reminiscences."

5. "Views and Reviews," *The Pittsburgh Courier*, July 3, 1926, p. 2. Frequently Schuyler lampooned black Americans who denied their blackness by claiming French, Indian, or other "exotic" blood. Du Bois, for example, is ridiculed in *Black No More* (see Chapter 5).

116 GEORGE S. SCHUYLER

6. "Editorial Notes," *The American Mercury*, 20 (August 1930).
7. Ibid.
8. See Chapter 4.
9. See "Reminiscences," pp. 146ff, 174.
10. For recent studies of the Harlem (or New Negro) Renaissance, see Arna Bontemps, ed., *The Harlem Renaissance Remembered* (New York: 1972); Nathan I. Huggins, *Harlem Renaissance* (New York, 1971); and Michael W. Peplow, and Arthur P. Davis, comps., *The New Negro Renaissance: An Anthology* (New York, 1975). For texts describing the Booker T. Washington attitude and the "new militancy" of Du Bois and other New Negroes, see August Meier, Elliott Rudwick, and Francis L. Broderick, eds., *Black Protest Thought in the Twentieth Century*, 2nd. ed. (Indianapolis, 1971). Also, see Chapter 2.
11. See Langston Hughes, "When the Negro Was in Vogue," *The Big Sea* (New York, 1940), pp. 223–33.
12. May 14, 1975 interview.
13. "Who's Who," *The Messenger*, 5 (June 1923), p. 748. The author of the statement is either Chandler Owen or A. Philip Randolph, co-editors of "The Only Radical Negro Magazine in America." *The Messenger's* combination of militant socialism, often savage satire, and inconoclastic attacks on the "elitism' of the NAACP and Du Bois, the overzealousness of Marcus Garvey, and the various idiocies of the Ku Klux Klan influenced Schuyler's philosophy and his writing style. For an account of A. Philip Randolph and his friendship with Schuyler, as well as an excellent history of *The Messenger* and the Harlem Renaissance leaders in general, see Jervis Anderson, *A. Philip Randolph: A Biographical Portrait* (New York, 1972).
14. "Hobohemia I: The World of the Migratory Worker," *The Messenger*, 5 (June 1923), pp. 741–44.
15. "Aframerican Fables," *The Messenger*, 6 (April, 1924), p. 108.
16. Ibid.
17. Ibid.
18. "This Simian World," *The Pittsburgh Courier*, November 22, 1924, p. 16.
19. "Thrusts and Lunges," *The Pittsburgh Courier*, January 27, 1925, p. 16.
20. "Views and Reviews," *The Pittsburgh Courier*, February 6, 1926, p. 3.
21. Quotations from "Speaking of Monuments and History" are from *The Pittsburgh Courier*, April 24, 1926, p. 16. Two months earlier, Schuyler said: "If we start such monuments . . . we'll have our children growing up full of pride in what their forefathers accomplished" ("Views and Reviews," *The Pittsburgh Courier*, January 27, 1925, p. 16).
22. "Aframerica Today," *The Pittsburgh Courier*, February 27, 1926, p. 3.
23. "Reminiscences," pp. 120–21.

24. One black scholar and Schuyler watcher told me that, except for Jack Johnson, the heavyweight boxing champion, Schuyler's was the first interracial "celebrity marriage" of this century. Interracial marriages were considered much more radical (and dangerous) in the early 1920s than they are now, primarily because of the number of states that had strict antimiscegenation laws—laws which Schuyler (understandably) campaigned against vigorously. His hope for an ultimate solution to the race problem through intermarriage is evident in "A Negro Looks Ahead" (see Chapter 3), in his many pamphlets and articles on racial intermarriage, and in *Black No More*. As he grew older, he became pessimistic about the chances of intermarriage transforming American society (see "Do Negroes Want to be White?", which is discussed in Chapter 3). In 1975 he told me "I have believed in integration and intermarriage for anyone who wants it. I didn't go around advocating it, because I didn't give a damn one way or another. [But] I still believe it is the solution" (May 14, 1975 interview).

25. No early venture of Schuyler's better illustrates his race pride than his campaign for the Young Negroes' Cooperative League. The uniqueness of his program, he told me in 1975, was that the league was "directed to the common man—the consumer—instead of the businessman." It "was to educate people to establish buying clubs and later to transform them into organizing societies." This "was something that appealed to a lot of young Negroes." Such leagues, he told me, "had worked all over the U.S. and abroad," and they "should have worked here in 1930."

Schuyler's league, however, was doomed from the start. He had no broad base of support. Funds were slow in coming in during a Depression year. And Schuyler had already alienated irrevocably the "old bourgeoisie," especially the conservative black businessmen who declared "war on Schuyler" (*The Pittsburgh Courier*, May 14, 1932, p. 6). Additionally, Schuyler cut his own throat a year later by publishing in *The American Mercury* his blistering attack on the Negro church—"Black America Begins to Doubt."

In retrospect, it is not hard to see that Schuyler had a very good idea, but that he alienated the wrong people and grew satiric at the wrong time. Not noted for his diplomacy, Schuyler needed every bit of good will he could get to make the Young Negroes' Cooperative League work. That he did not get that good will is partly the fault of the essential conservatism of business and partly the fault of his own iconoclasm.

26. "Reminiscences," pp. 88–90. See also *Black and Conservative*, pp. 198–204.

27. "Reminiscences," p. 96.

28. For a concise history, see Peter M. and Mort N. Bergman, comps., *The Chronological History of the Negro in America* (New York, 1969), pp. 453–55.

29. For Schuyler's later views on McCarthy, see Chapter 7.

30. Schuyler was investigating one J. Livert Kelly in Chicago. In a letter

to Robert L. Vann of *The Pittsburgh Courier* (June 8, 1938), Schuyler described the episode: "Kelly's mob" knows "I am in town, and they are suspicious and uneasy. . . . I was talking to a tavern proprietor Kelly had shaken down . . . when who should come in the door but Kelly." The tavern owner introduced the journalist to the mobster: "Kelly was taken aback. I watched him closely for a move for his gun, since his usual tactic is to whip people over the head with his pistol. He said: 'You've been opening your mouth pretty wide not to know what you're talking about. I don't like people that open their mouths too wide.' To which I replied: 'No, neither do I,' and looked him in the eye, sternly and unsmilingly. He paused for a minute, then turned on his heel and walked out without another word." See *Black and Conservative*, pp. 243–44. Schuyler adds that "investigating this fellow did not add to my peace of mind while I was in Chicago" (Ibid., p. 246).

31. Letter dated January 16, 1974. Philippa was the *Manchester Union Leader's* correspondent in Africa and Asia during the 1960s until she was killed in Viet Nam while ferrying orphaned children back from the front; the helicopter crashed, and she and one of the orphans were killed. Philippa had been a child prodigy, a concert pianist of extraordinary talent, and an author. See *Time*, 27 (June 22, 1936), p. 40; *Time*, 36 (July 1, 1940), p. 48; and *The New Yorker*, 16 (August 31, 1940), p. 28. She wrote *Adventures in Black and White* and *Who Killed the Congo?*

32. Letter dated January 16, 1974. Loeb mentioned Schuyler's and Philippa's role at the *Manchester Union Leader* on the "David Susskind" show, PBS (June 16, 1975).

33. West, p. C-1.

34. Ibid.

35. May 14, 1975 interview.

Chapter Two

1. W.E.B. Du Bois, "The Browsing Reader," *The Crisis*, 38 (January 1931), p. 16. Du Bois wrote this piece to praise Schuyler for having just published "Black Warriors" in *The American Mercury*.

2. Robert Bone in *The Negro Novel in America* and Charles Larson in his "Introduction" to *Black No More* use these phrases to describe Schuyler. Both refer to or quote passages from "The Negro-Art Hokum" to support their contentions (see Chapter 5).

3. See Huggins, chs. 4 and 5; and Peplow and Davis, sec. 8, for a discussion of the critical debate that occurred during the 1920s. Schuyler's "The Negro-Art Hokum" and Langston Hughes' "The Negro Artist and the Racial Mountain" are included in the Peplow and Davis anthology. Selections from *The Crisis* symposium, "The Negro in Art: How Shall He Be Portrayed?" are also included.

4. Ralph W. Bullock, *In Spite of Handicaps* (New York, 1927), p. 31.

5. Peplow and Davis organize their anthology according to seven major

Harlem Renaissance themes: "Protest Literature"; "The Genteel School: We Are Like You . . ."; "Nigger Heaven: Variations on a Theme"; "The African Heritage"; "About the Folk"; "Race Pride"; and "The Stirrings of Black Nationalism."

6. Hughes' essay was not written specifically as an answer to Schuyler, though many critics have assumed it was. For that matter, as Schuyler and others have noted, Hughes' essay did not even address itself directly to Schuyler's comments. Hughes just "didn't join issue at all," said Schuyler in "Reminiscences," p. 78.

7. Langston Hughes, "The Negro Artist and the Racial Mountain," *The Nation*, 122 (June 23, 1926), p. 694.

8. Booker T. Washington's "Atlanta Exposition Address" (1895) was a good example of the old accommodationism: "The wisest among my race understand that the agitation of the race question is the extremest folly . . ." The Du Boisian concept of the new militancy was exemplified in "The Niagara Statement" (1905), the NAACP's "First Statement of Purpose" (1910), and in "Returning Soldiers." In the latter piece Du Bois said: "By the God of heaven, we are cowards and jackasses if now that the war is over, we do not marshall every ounce of our brain and brawn to fight a sterner, longer, more unending battle against the forces of hell in our own land." W.E.B. Du Bois, "Returning Soldiers," *The Crisis*, 17, (January 1920), p. 107. For these and other documents, see Peplow and Davis, pp. 402–61; Meier et. al., pp. 245–295, and Daniel Walden, ed., *W. E. B. Du Bois: The Crisis Writings* (New York, 1972).

9. *The Messenger*, 6 (October, 1924), p. 322.

10. *The Messenger*, 6 (December, 1924), pp. 384–85.

11. *The Messenger*, 7 (August, 1925), p. 297. Schuyler said later: ". . . we also used to bait Kelly Miller and others who, we thought, were not radical enough . . . in their approach. . . . These people . . . were too conservative, or in some instances too reactionary" ("Reminiscences," pp. 79–80).

12. These authors are praised in his "Views and Reviews" columns in *The Pittsburgh Courier*—July 19, 1930, p. 10; May 17, 1930, p. 10; September 13, 1930, p. 10; and February 6, 1932, p. 10. Johnson was one of the spiritual mentors of the Harlem Renaissance whom Schuyler greatly admired (see "Reminiscences," p. 118); J. A. Rogers, a fellow columnist at *The Messenger*, did much to educate Schuyler in the black American and African heritages. Eugene Huffman's satire, *Now I Am Civilized*, was effective, according to Schuyler, because in it "the fads and foibles and shortcomings of white and black folk are held up with more or less effectiveness to the mirror of ridicule" (February 6, 1932)—something Schuyler did in *Black No More*. Wallace Thurman's *Infants of the Spring* was "sadistically amusing, sometimes prankish, and always objectively observant" because the author takes "vicious jabs" at the black bourgeoisie, white racists, and liberal whites "who make a fad of cultivating a group of Negro friends and 'helping the Negro race' " (February 6, 1932).

13. "Views and Reviews," *The Pittsburgh Courier*, July 26, 1930, p. 10.

14. See *Black and Conservative*, p. 157; and "Reminiscences," pp. 76–78.

15. "The Negro-Art Hokum," *The Nation*, 122 (June 16, 1926), p. 662; further references are given in the text.

16. "Negroes and Artists," *The Nation*, 123 (July 24, 1926), p. 36. The following quotations are from this letter to the editor.

17. "Views and Reviews," *The Pittsburgh Courier*, July 3, 1926, p. 2. Benjamin Brawley, one of the foremost black critics of the 1920s and 1930s, puts the whole argument in perspective in *The Negro Genius* (New York, 1937), pp. 11–15.

18. "Views and Reviews," *The Pittsburgh Courier*, August 30, 1930, p. 10.

19. Ibid. Years later Malcolm X said that white Christians have taught blacks to "keep our eyes fixed on the pie in the sky . . . while [they] enjoy [their] heaven right here . . . on *this* earth." See *The Autobiography of Malcolm X* (New York, 1964), pp. 200–201.

Chapter Three

1. "The Negro and Nordic Civilization," *The Messenger*, 7 (May 1925), p. 198. Further references will be given in the text.

2. "Blessed Are the Sons of Ham," *The Nation*, 124 (March 23, 1927), p. 313. Further references will be given in the text.

3. H. L. Mencken wrote Schuyler about another piece and warned him not to overdue the attack: "Here again, it seems to me, you spoil a good story by showing too much indignation. . . . Thus the general effect of the article is considerably diminished. . . . In such writing . . . the really effective weapon is irony. The moment you begin to show indignation you weaken your whole case." Guy J. Forgue, ed., *Letters of H. L. Mencken* (New York, 1961), p. 349.

Schuyler and Mencken became friends in 1927 and corresponded through 1939. Many critics have noted that Schuyler's style was Menckenesque; indeed, their philosophies were similar on a number of issues, for both of them were iconoclasts (see Chapter 8). Mencken once wrote the NAACP's Walter White to tell him to listen more carefully to what Schuyler had to say on a given issue (Forgue, pp. 478–79). And he wrote Blanche Knopf in 1937 to tell her that "there is an excellent book in George S. Schuyler . . . the best writer the Negroes have ever produced, and . . . he is a highly intelligent man. . . . He loves to tell the truth" (Forgue, p. 419).

4. See W. E. B. Du Bois, "The Browsing Reader," *The Crisis*, 39 (March 1931), p. 100, where the editor says that *Black No More* "carries not

only scathing criticism of Negro leaders, but of the mass of Negroes, and then it passes over and slaps the white people just as hard and unflinchingly straight in the face." Schuyler's habit of attacking the weaknesses of one race, then crossing over and attacking the weaknesses of the other race, was established early in his career.

5. "Our White Folks," *The American Mercury*, 12 (December 1927), p. 385. Further references will be given in the text. The italicized passages show that Schuyler was still convinced that we are living in an "insane asylum," a typical satiric premise that Schuyler might have inherited from Jonathan Swift, whom he greatly admired.

6. "Our Greatest Gift to America," in Charles S. Johnson, ed., *Ebony and Topaz: A Collectanea* (New York, 1927), p. 122. Further references will be given in the text.

7. Melvin B. Tolson, "George S. Schuyler," *The American Mercury*, 28 (March 1933), pp. 373–74.

8. "A Negro Looks Ahead," *The American Mercury*, 19 (February 1930), p. 212. Further references will be given in the text. Mencken had written to Schuyler in 1929 that "the plain fact is that neither the whites nor the blacks know where they are heading. . . . I can never formulate a plausible picture of the relation of the races . . . fifty years from now. If you care to deal with the subject realistically, I'll certainly be delighted to do the article" (Forgue, p. 313).

9. "The Caucasion Problem," in Rayford Logan, ed., *What The Negro Wants* (Chapel Hill, 1944), p. 281. Further references will be given in the text.

10. The "cultured hell" reference recalls Claude McKay's poem, "America."

11. "Do Negroes Want to be White?" *The American Mercury*, 82 (June 1956), p. 56. Further reference will be given in the text.

12. "Our nation is moving toward two societies, one black, one white— separate and unequal. . . . Discrimination and segregation have long permeated much of American life; they now threaten the future of every American. This deepening racial division is not inevitable. The movement apart can be reversed. Choice is still possible. Our principal task is to define that choice and to press for a national resolution. To pursue our present course will involve the continuing polarization of the American community and, ultimately, the destruction of basic democratic values. . . ." "Summary," *Report of the National Advisory Commission on Civil Disorders* (New York, 1968), p. 1.

Chapter Four

1. Tolson, pp. 373–74.
2. "Shafts and Darts," *The Messenger*, 8 (September 1926), p. 271.

Schuyler said later: "I wrote doggeral and things of that sort . . . if I felt the subject called for that kind of treatment." But I "was adapting a style which was in keeping with the subject matter . . . I think a writer has to have some sort of versatility." The later pieces "called for a story-telling narrative. . . ." See "Reminiscences," p. 274.

3. "At the Coffeehouse," *The Messenger*, 7 (June 1925), p. 237.

4. "The Yellow Peril," *The Messenger*, 7 (January 1925), p. 28. Further references will be given in the text.

5. The heroine's comment underscores another Schuyler cause not yet mentioned: women's rights. "I'd always been a feminist from the beginning . . . [and] favored the general revolt of women which culminated in the 19th Amendment" ("Reminiscences," p. 66).

6. See Chapter 5 for a definition of the *picaro*-trickster tradition.

7. "Seldom Seen," *The Messenger*, 8 (November 1926), pp. 342–44; 347. Further references will be given in the text.

8. Schuyler told me during our May 1975 interview that the character of Seldom Seen "definitely anticipated and probably influenced" the character of Max.

9. "Reminiscences," p. 275.

10. "Black Warriors," *The American Mercury*, 21 (November 1930), pp. 288–97. Further references will be given in the text.

11. "Memoirs of a Pearl Diver," *The American Mercury*, 22 (April 1931), pp. 487–496. Further references will be given in the text.

12. "Black Art," *The American Mercury*, 27 (November 1932), pp. 335–42. Further references will be given in the text. Additional recollections about his grandmother appear in *Black and Conservative*, pp. 20–24.

13. Schuyler later recalled that Hurston was "one of the soundest writers of the Harlem Renaissance. . . . She seemed to have her feet on the ground, . . . because she was earthy and a product of the earth; she wrote about what she knew, and if it didn't always present the Negro as a Bond-street tailored gentleman or a Paris-gowned lady, well . . . she wasn't ashamed of it" ("Reminiscences," pp. 117–18). Schuyler contrasted her genuine love of folklore and the folk with the "bohemian" attitude of some Harlem Renaissance authors. Hurston's "Eatonville Anthology," incidentally, was published in *The Messenger* while Schuyler was on the staff. It influenced him just as surely as the work of J. A. Rogers, another staffer, influenced his respect for the black American and African heritage.

14. Tolson, p. 373. Further references will be given in the text.

15. See Joy Flasch, *Melvin B. Tolson* (New York, 1972), pp. 27 and 29. Schuyler told me he had heard about the dramatization but had never seen it.

Chapter Five

1. Du Bois, "The Browsing Reader," *The Crisis*, 39 (March 1931), p. 100.

2. Calverton also "was instrumental in getting the Macaulay Company to publish it." See *Black and Conservative*, p, 170. Calverton, editor of *The Modern Quarterly* (later, *The Modern Monthly*), had already published Schuyler's "Our Greatest Gift to America" and "Emancipated Woman and the Negro."

3. Gilbert Highet, *The Anatomy of Satire* (Princeton, 1962), p. 158. Satire "is topical," says Highet, and "it claims to be realistic (although it is usually exaggerated or distorted)" (Ibid., p. 5).

4. *Black No More* (New York, 1971), "Dedication." Further references will be given in the text. Schuyler's basic story about a discovery that turns black skin white, incidentally, had a literary antecedent of which he was unaware. In "Eureka," a black poet named J. Mord Allen "imagines that an inexpensive medical preparation has been discovered which, upon inges-tion, immediately endows all Negroes with a white skin and straight hair." The poem—a satire—was published in 1906. I am indebted to Jean Wagner (pp. 143–44) for having spotted this early use of the motif. Another antecedent was an article by Schuyler's old enemy, Kelly Miller, entitled "Is the American Negro to Remain Black or Become Bleached?" in *South Atlantic Quarterly*, 25 (July 1926), pp. 240–52.

5. Schuyler constantly protested the skin-whitening and hair-straightening advertisements that appeared in black publications: "No matter how inoffensively the skin-whitening advertisements in Negro newspapers are worded to spare the embarrassment of the more sensitive readers, they are there and in profusion . . . opposite flaming editorials extolling pride in blackness." See *Black and Conservative*, p. 123. Exam-ples of these advertisements—from *The Pittsburgh Courier* (March 29, 1929 and November 2, 1929)—are as follows: "Amazing New Bleach Cream Discovered: Whitens Skin 7 Shades in 7 Nights or MONEY BACK"; "You can safely and quickly whiten your skin and have a clearer, lighter com-plexion that everyone envies and admires . . . with FAN TAN"; "Dr. Fred Palmer's Skin Whitener"; "Golden Peacock Bleach Creme"; "Mme. C. J. Walker's TAN-OFF will bleach the blemishes out of your skin"; "If you use PLUKO Hair Dressing, your hair will be softer, straighter and more radiantly beautiful." One advertisement probably directly inspired Schuyler: "Pour some SPANOLA Whitening Fluid on the palms of your hands and give yourself a *quick, one-minute massage. Instantly,* the color of your skin will turn to a lovely creamy-white. . . . Your friends will be amazed and delighted with the change and will ask you what you have done to make such *an improvement*" (my italics). This advertisement appeared in an issue in which Schuyler took Dr. Noguchi to task (see note 6).

6. "Racial Metamorphosis Claimed by Scientist: Japanese Says He Can Change Black Skin Into White," *The Pittsburgh Courier*, November 2, 1929, p. 1. Schuyler's column for that day was devoted to the news story and appeared on p. 12 of the same issue. Said Schuyler: "Truly a moment-ous not to say financially profitable discovery. I have been prophesying it for

some years and have even written something built around such a discovery [i.e., a first draft of *Black No More?*]. . . . If our cosmetic companies are wise, they will immediately pay some of our Negro biologists to go to Japan and study under Professor Noguchi so they won't be entirely put out of business when the serum or treatment is exploited in this country."

7. See Wallace Thurman's *The Blacker the Berry*.

8. Similar nightclub scenes, involving savage passions, hot jazz, wild lovemaking, and an inevitable fight over a woman may be found in any of the "Harlem Vogue" novels, including Carl Van Vechten's *Nigger Heaven* and Claude McKay's *Home to Harlem*. That parties of "slumming whites" went to Harlem during the 1920s is verified by newspaper reports of " 'Ofay' Parties Filling Harlem Nightclubs: Nordics, Seeking New Diversion, Once More Turn To Colored New York To Find Thrills," *The Pittsburgh Courier*, July 26, 1930, p. II-6.

9. That Max "passes over" is probably a reference to another school of literature that Schuyler mocked—passing literature. In these stories the heroine or hero is light enough to pass as white and "crosses over the line" to live in the white world. See James Weldon Johnson's *The Autobiography of an Ex-Coloured Man*, Walter White's *Flight*, Jessie Fauset's *Plum Bun*, and Nella Larsen's *Passing*. Often, miscegenation occurs in these works; in *Black No More*, Max of course marries Helen, the white girl from the South, after he "passes over." The best known treatment of the miscegenation motif in the 1920s was *All God's Chillun Got Wings* by Eugene O'Neill. O'Neill's play did not involve "passing," however. Schuyler told me in May 1975 that he "definitely wanted to spoof these novels and other works" involving the color line, especially to show just how fragile (and ridiculous) the concept of separation of the races is in practice.

10. See the famous "hospital scene" (Chapter 11) in Ralph Ellison's *Invisible Man*, (New York, 1952), where the young hero is reborn.

11. Highet, p. 158.

12. That Santop Licorice (Garvey) was not invited is a mocking reference to the famous feud between Marcus Garvey and W.E.B. Du Bois in the early 1920s. Arthur P. Davis describes a scene he witnessed in the 1920s when Garvey and Du Bois walked past each other in Harlem without acknowledging each other's existence. See "Harlem During the New Negro Renaissance," *The Oracle* (Summer 1971), pp. 3–8.

13. See W.E.B. Du Bois, "The Black Mother," *The Crisis*, 5 (December 1912), p. 78.

14. That Du Bois romanticized Africa is evident even more in "The Story of Africa," *The Crisis*, 8 (September 1914), pp. 234–35. Beard's reference to "To your tents, O Israel" makes Schuyler seem prophetic: Du Bois published an essay of that name in *The Crisis*, 39 (March 1932), pp. 93–94, one year after the appearance of *Black No More*.

15. Du Bois was amused by the character of Dr. Beard: "You are bound to enjoy it [the novel] and to follow with joyous laughter the adventures of

Max Disher and Bunny, Dr. Crookman and —we say it with all reservations—Dr. Shakespeare Agamemnon Beard." *The Crisis*, 39 (March 1931), p. 100. Nor did Schuyler dislike Du Bois. He said years later that though Du Bois was not "a friend or crony . . . I found him a pretty witty person" ("Reminiscences," p. 247).

16. See Bergman, pp. 256–57.

17. Hughes, *The Big Sea*, p. 244.

18. *The Crisis*, 39 (March 1931), p. 100.

19. "I didn't have particular men in mind for characters like McPhule, Kretin, Handen Moutthe, and Buggerie," Schuyler told me in May 1975, "but they were the types that were in the news every day."

20. See "The Various Shady Lives of the Ku Klux Klan," in John Hope Franklin and Isidore Starr, eds., *The Negro in Twentieth Century America* (New York, 1967), pp. 187–91. Schuyler frequently attacked Simmons in *The Messenger* and *The Pittsburgh Courier*.

21. Ibid.

22. See *The Pittsburgh Courier*, March 1, 1924, p. 15.

23. The National States Rights Party, for example, still publishes *The Thunderbolt: The White Man's Viewpoint* and disseminates a libelous tract entitled "Negro and Ape."

24. See Bone, pp. 89–94.

25. See Gilbert Osofsky, "A Note on the Usefulness of Folklore" in Gilbert Osofsky, ed., *Puttin' on Ole Massa* (New York, 1969), pp. 45–48, for a description of this tradition in the slave narratives.

26. C. Hugh Holman, *A Handbook to Literature*. 3rd edition (New York, 1972), pp. 391–92.

27. Ibid.

28. Ulrich Wicks, "The Nature of Picaresque Narrative: A Modal Approach," *PMLA*, 89 (March 1974), p. 242.

29. Ibid. In *Black No More*, the "chaotic landscape" is caused by Black-No-More, Inc., and by the activities of Max and Bunny in the South, both of whom put the country on the defensive.

30. Ibid., pp. 244–45.

31. For Fauset's essay on "American Negro Folk Literature" and some of the tales he recorded, see Locke, pp. 238–49. For Zora Neale Hurston's influence on Schuyler, see note 13, Chapter 4. Other authors and scholars also preserved folklore—Charles W. Chesnutt and Thomas W. Talley, for example.

32. William Schechter, *The History of Negro Humor in America* (New York, 1970), pp. 52–53. Two earlier examples of rural tricksters appear in "The Passing of Grandison" and *The Conjure Woman* by Charles W. Chesnutt. A good example of the urban trickster is Sam Lucas in Countee Cullen's *One Way to Heaven*.

33. Other studies and anthologies on black folklore, humor, and satire that I found especially helpful include Joyce Nower, "Foolin' Master,"

Satire News Letter, 7 (1969), pp. 5–9; Langston Hughes and Arna Bontemps, eds., *The Book of Negro Folklore* (New York, 1959); Langston Hughes, ed., *The Book of Negro Humor* (New York, 1966); Alan Dundes, ed., *Mother Wit from the Laughing Barrel* (Englewood Cliffs, 1973); and Roger Rosenblatt, *Black Fiction* (Cambridge, Mass., 1974).

34. "As a boy," Max "had been taught to look up to white folks as just a little less than gods" (63). This attitude changes drastically in the course of the novel.

35. When Helen became pregnant the first time, Bunny—with Max's tacit approval—burned down her home in order to force her to go to a Crookman sanitorium to have her baby. Neither *picaro* seems especially upset when she loses the baby because of the trauma. With this background, we can only raise an eyebrow at Max's confession. Maybe Schuyler wanted Max to be a more chivalrous hero—at least for a moment.

36. See Michael W. Peplow, "George Schuyler, Satirist: Rhetorical Devices in *Black No More*," *CLA Journal*, 18 (December 1974), pp. 242–57.

37. See Highet, pp. 3–23.

38. Like other iconoclasts such as Mencken, Schuyler attacked the Southern Christian mentality ferociously; see "Southern White Christianity," *The Pittsburgh Courier*, August 10, 1929, pp. 1–12.

39. Alexander Pope, *The Dunciad*, Book IV, lines 649–56. See John Butt, ed., *The Poems of Alexander Pope* (New Haven: Single-volume edition of the Twickenham Text, 1963), p. 800.

40. W.O.S. Sutherland, *The Art of the Satirist* (Austin, 1965), p. 10.

41. Holman, p. 279.

42. During our May 1975 interview, Schuyler wouldn't identify the actual physician he was satirizing; he was, Schuyler admitted, "a very capable surgeon" of the time.

43. The implications of this passage are rather curious, seeing as Schuyler too had a white wife and had written in defense of interracial marriage.

44. Arthur P. Davis, "Black Satire," *Opportunity*, 9 (March 1931), p. 89.

45. W.E.B. Du Bois, "The Browsing Reader," *The Crisis*, 39 (March 1931), p. 100.

46. Alain Locke, "We Turn to Prose: A Retrospective Review of the Literature of the Negro for 1931," *Opportunity*, 10 (February 1932), p. 43.

47. Sterling A. Brown, *The Negro in American Fiction* (1937; reprinted New York, 1969), p. 145.

48. Davis, "Black Satire," p. 89.

49. Rudolph Fisher, *Books* (February 1931), 5.

50. "A Satire on Color," *The New York Times Book Review* (February 1, 1931), p. 9.

51. H.L. Mencken, "Check List of New Books," *The American Mercury*, 22 (April 1931), n.p.

52. Dorothy Van Doren, "Black, Alas, No More!" *The Nation*, 132 (February 25, 1931), pp. 218–19. Mrs. Schuyler responded (Schuyler was out of the country) in *The Nation*, 132 (April 8, 1931), p. 132.

53. Bone, pp. 89ff.

54. Ibid.

55. Ibid.

56. Ibid.

57. Charles Larson, "Introduction," p. 10. Further references will be given in the text.

58. Janheinz Janz, *Neo-African Literature* (New York, 1969), pp. 199–200.

59. Ruth Miller, ed., *Blackamerican Literature* (Beverly Hills, 1971), p. 381.

60. Carl Milton Hughes, *The Negro Novelist* (New York, 1953), p. 37. The book was also praised by Hugh M. Gloster, *Negro Fiction in the United States* (New York, 1948), pp. 189–90.

61. Davis, *From the Dark Tower*, pp. 104–08.

62. Ishmael Reed, *Shrovetide in Old New Orleans* (Garden City, 1978), p. 195. The Schuyler interview was conducted in October 1972 and first published in *Yardbird II* in 1973.

63. John Pfeiffer, "Black American Speculative Fiction: A Checklist," *Extrapolation: A Journal of Science Fiction and Fantasy*, 17 (December 1975), pp. 36–39.

64. Ivor A. Rogers, "The Gernsback Era, 1926–1937," in Neil Barron, ed., *Anatomy of Wonder: Science Fiction* (New York, 1976), p. 110.

Chapter Six

1. *Black and Conservative*, p. 186.

2. Ibid. The only previous work by a black American author on Africa was Henry F. Downing's *The American Cavalryman: A Liberian Romance;* portions of it were set in the United States, however.

3. See "Uncle Sam Strikes a Moral Pose" and "League of Nations Sidesteps Liberian Issue," *The Pittsburgh Courier*, January 31, 1931, pp. I-2 and I-5. Coverage of the Liberia issue continued weekly in the black press for almost two years.

4. For background works and anthologies on the Harlem Renaissance, see Chapter 1, note 10.

5. See, for example, Africanus Schaack's comments in *The Negro World* (July 11, 1931), a Garveyite publication, which were reprinted in *The Pittsburgh Courier* (July 18, 1931) p. II-1 under "Heated War on Liberia Rages: Editor Schaack Takes Schuyler to Task. . . ." Schaack said: "Mr. Schuyler looks at Liberia first as a WHITE man, secondly as an American, thirdly as a Christian, fourthly as a Puritan, and fifthly as one who is peeved

at the fever he 'caught.' " Schuyler answered in the same issue with similar spirit: "Certain . . . woozy fellows have risen up in idiotic criticism of my . . . [articles]. . . ." Other articles of interest: "Schuyler Too Severe on the Missionaries in His Liberia Report" in *The Pittsburgh Courier* (July 25, 1931), p. II-10, and "Schuyler Arouses Ire of Africans at Mass Meeting" in *The Pittsburgh Courier* (August 15, 1931), p. I-1.

    6. See "Reminiscences," pp. 261–67, 272–73.

    7. John M. Harrison and Harry H. Stein, eds., *Muckraking: Past, Present, and Future* (University Park, Pa., 1973), p. 14. Black muckrakers during the Harlem Renaissance included W.E.B. Du Bois and Walter White, Chandler Owen and A. Philip Randolph. See Nathan I. Huggins, *Harlem Renaissance*, pp. 28–29.

    8. Schuyler's articles appeared between September 12 and October 31, 1931, in *The Pittsburgh Courier*.

    9. *The Pittsburgh Courier*, October 3, 1931, p. II-6.

    10. Ibid.

    11. *The Pittsburgh Courier*, October 17, 1931, p. II-6.

    12. *The Pittsburgh Courier*, October 31, 1931, p. II-6.

    13. *Slaves Today: A Story of Liberia* (New York, 1931), p. 243. Further references will be given in the text.

    14. See James Ngugi, "Satire in Nigeria: Chinua Achebe, T. M. Aluko and Wole Soyinka," in Cosmo Pieterse and Donald Munro, eds., *Protest and Conflict in African Literature* (New York, 1969), and Michael W. Peplow, "The Black White Man in African Protest Literature," *The Lock Haven Review*, 13 (1972), pp. 3–14.

    15. H.L. Mencken, "Checklist of New Books," *The American Mercury*, 25 (February 1932), n.p.

    16. "Dark Slaves of Liberia," reprinted in *The Pittsburgh Courier*, January 2, 1932, p. 10.

    17. Ibid.

    18. Dewey R. Jones, "Slaves Today," *Opportunity*, 10 (January 1932), 27.

    19. Mary W. Ovington, "Book Chat," *The Pittsburgh Courier*, February 1947. (15-page pamphlet)
6, 1932, p. II-2.

    20. "Liberia Today," *The New York Times Book Review*, December 27, 1931, p. 9.

    21. Davis, *From the Dark Tower*, pp. 106–107. Robert Bone, Nathan Huggins and Arna Bontemps in their studies of the Harlem Renaissance do not mention *Slaves Today* at all.

    22. October, 1973 interview.

Chapter Seven

    1. Larson, p. 13.

    2. *Black and Conservative*, pp. 49–50. Further references will be given in the text.

3. Davis, *From the Dark Tower*, p. 107.

4. Ralph Ellison, *Invisible Man* (New York, 1946), chs. 13 ff, where the protagonist first joins and then attempts to escape "the Brotherhood."

5. *The Pittsburgh Courier* refused to publish Schuyler's article on Martin Luther King, so it was published by William Loeb in the *Manchester Union Leader*, November 10, 1964, p. 1.

6. "Malcolm X: Better to Memorialize Benedict Arnold," *American Opinion* (February 1973), p. 36. Schuyler sent me a copy of this article along with a note saying that I "might get a chuckle out of it."

Chapter Eight

1. Du Bois, "The Browsing Reader," *The Crisis*, 39 (March 1931), p. 89. "The Forethought," *The Souls of Black Folk* (Chicago, 1903), n.p.

2. Locke, "We Turn to Prose: A Retrospective Review of the Literature of the Negro for 1931," *Opportunity*, 10 (February 1932), p. 43.

3. Gloster, p. 187.

4. Davis, *From the Dark Tower*, p. 108.

5. Ibid., p. 106.

6. Gloster, pp. 189–190.

7. Davis, *From the Dark Tower*, p. 105.

8. Anderson, p. 144.

9. *The Crisis*, 72 (October 1965), pp. 484–85.

10. Ernest J. Hopkins, comp., *The Enlarged Devil's Dictionary* (Garden City, 1967), p. 141. Hopkin's introductory essay, "Bierce, the Caustic Columnist," is excellent.

11. J.D. Shaw, ed., *Brann the Iconoclast*, 2 vols. (Waco, Texas, 1898), p. 124. For a description of Brann's career, see Shaw's introduction. I am indebted to Mr. Robert S. Bravard for suggestions concerning the "peculiarly American tradition" of journalistic iconoclasm and for noting the parallels between Brann's style and Schuyler's.

12. Ibid., p. 7.

13. Mencken defines the term in *A Mencken Chrestomathy* (New York, 1949), p. 17.

14. Ibid.

15. Larson, p. 13.

Selected Bibliography

PRIMARY SOURCES

1. Novels, Monographs, and Autobiography

Black and Conservative: The Autobiography of George S. Schuyler. New Rochelle: New York: Arlington House, 1966; rpt. 1971.

Black No More: Being an Account of the Strange and Wonderful Workings of Science in the Land of the Free, A.D. 1933–1940. New York: The Macaulay Company, 1931; rpt. New York: "African-American Library" Series, The Macmillan Company, 1971; Washington, D.C.: The Consortium Press, n.d.

The Communist Conspiracy Against the Negroes. New York: Catholic Information Society, 1947. (16-page pamphlet)

Fifty Years of Progress in Negro Journalism. Pittsburgh: The Pittsburgh Courier Publishing Company, 1950. (7-page pamphlet)

The Red Drive in the Colonies. New York: Catholic Information Society, 1947 (15-page pamphlet)

Slaves Today: A Story of Liberia. New York: Brewer, Warren and Putnam, 1931; rpt. AMS Press, New York, 1969; Washington, D.C. The Consortium Press, n.d.

2. Short Stories, Essays, Reviews, and Articles

"America Caught Up With Him." *The Crisis,* 49 (June 1942), 194–95.

"At the Coffeehouse." *The Messenger,* 7 (June 1925), 236–37.

"At the Darktown Charity Ball." *The Messenger,* 6 (December 1924), 377–78.

"Black America Begins to Doubt." *The American Mercury,* 25 (April 1932), 423–30.

"Black Art." *The American Mercury,* 27 (November 1932), 335–42.

"Black No More." *Negro Digest,* 8 (April 1950), 64–69 (an excerpt from the novel of the same name).

"Black Paradise Lost." *Opportunity,* 13 (April 1935), 113–16.

"Black Warriors." *The American Mercury,* 21 (November 1930), 288–97.

"Blessed Are the Organized." *The Messenger,* 8 (November 1926), 347.

"Blessed Are the Sons of Ham." *The Nation,* 124 (March 23, 1927), 313–315.

"The Caucasian Problem." In Rayford Logan, ed., *What the Negro Wants.* Chapel Hill: The University of North Carolina Press, 1944.

"Craftsman in the Blue Grass." *The Crisis*, 47 (May 1940), 143 and 157–58.

"Do Negroes Want to be White?" *The American Mercury*, 82 (June 1956), 55–60.

"Do We Really Want Equality?" *The Crisis*, 44 (April 1937), 102–103.

"Dr. Jekyll and Mr. Hyde and the Negro." In Sylvestre C. Watkins, ed., *Anthology of American Negro Literatare*. New York: Random House, 1944.

"Emancipated Woman and the Negro." *The Modern Quarterly*, 5 (Fall 1929), 361–63. Reprinted in the Little Blue Book Series.

"Freedom of the Press in Mississippi." *The Crisis*, 43 (October 1936), 302–303 and 306.

"Freedom Through Finance." *Sepia*, 11 (May 1962), 55–58.

"From Job to Job." *The World Tomorrow* (April 1923).

"Forty Years of 'The Crisis'." *The Crisis*, 58 (March 1951), 163–64.

"Garner at Home." *The Crisis*, 47 (June 1940), 170–71 and 178.

"Haiti Looks Ahead." *por Américas*, 1 (December 1949), 6–8.

"Hitlerism without Hitler: A Review." *The Crisis*, 48 (December 1941), 384 and 389.

"Hobohemia I: The World of the Migratory Worker." *The Messenger*, 5 (June 1923), 741–44.

"Hobohemia II: The Folk Farthest Down." *The Messenger*, 5 (August 1923), 787–88 and 796–99.

"Jim Crow in the North." *The American Mercury*, 68 (June 1949), 663–70.

"John A. Lankford." *The Messenger*, 6 (June 1924), 192–93.

"Keeping the Negro in his Place." *The American Mercury*, 17 (August 1929), 469–76.

"Krushchev's African Foothold." *The American Mercury*, 88 (March 1959) 57–49.

"A Long War will Aid the Negro." *The Crisis*, 50 (November 1943), 328–29 and 344.

"The Lord's Work." *Globe* (July 1937).

"Madam C. J. Walker." *The Messenger*, 6 (August 1924), 251–58, 264, and 266.

"Malcolm X: Better to Memorialize Benedict Arnold." *American Opinion* (February 1973), 31–36.

"Memoirs of a Pearl Diver." *The American Mercury*, 22 (April 1931), 487–96.

"Monrovia Mooches On." *Globe* (July 1937).

"More Race Riots are Coming." *The American Mercury*, 59 (December 1944), 686–91.

"Mortimer M. Harris." *The Messenger*, 6 (May 1924), 140–44.

"The Negro-Art Hokum." *The Nation*, 122 (June 16, 1926), 662–63.

"The Negro in the New Order." *The Modern Quarterly*, 11 (Fall 1940), 85–87.

"A Negro Looks Ahead." *The American Mercury*, 19 (February 1930), 212–20. Excerpted in *Review of Reviews*, 81 (March 1930), 91.

"The Negro and Nordic Civilization." *The Messenger*, 7 (May 1925), 198–201 and 207.

"The Negro Press." *The New Leader* (June 26, 1943).

"The Negro Voter Comes of Age." *The American Mercury*, 84 (March 1957), 99–104.

"Negroes and Artists: A Letter." *The Nation*, 123 (July 24, 1926), 36.

"Negroes Reject Communism." *The American Mercury*, 47 (June 1939), 176–81.

"New Job Frontiers for Negro Youth." *The Crisis*, 43 (November 1936), 328–29.

"Not Gone With the Wind." *The Crisis*, 44 (July 1937), 205–206.

"Our Greatest Gift to America." In Charles S. Johnson, ed., *Ebony and Topaz, A Collectanea*. New York: Opportunity, 1927. Reprinted in V. F. Calverton, ed., *Anthology of American Negro Literature*. New York: Modern Library, 1929.

"Our White Folks." *The American Mercury*, 12 (December 1927), 385–92. Excerpted in *Review of Reviews*, 77 (January 1928), 93–94.

"The Phantom American Negro." *Reader's Digest*, 59 (July 1951), 61–63.

"Racial Intermarriage in the United States." *The American Parade*, 1 (Fall 1928). Reprinted as Little Blue Book Number 1387.

"Reflections on Negro Leadership." *The Crisis*, 44 (November 1937), 327–28 and 347.

"The Reminiscences of George S. Schuyler." New York: Oral History Collection of Columbia University, 1960.

"Richetta G. Randolph." *The Crisis*, 49 (December 1942), 382 and 396.

"The Rise of the Black Internationale." *The Crisis*, 45 (August 1938), 255–57, 274–75, and 277.

"Scripture for Lynchers." *The Crisis*, 42 (January 1935), 12.

"Seldom Seen." *The Messenger*, 8 (November 1926), 342–44 and 347.

"The Separate State Hokum." *The Crisis*, 42 (May 1935), 135 and 148–49.

"Some Unsweet Truths about Race Prejudice." In Samuel D. Schmalhausen, ed., *Behold America*. New York: Farrar and Rinehart, 1931.

"Teaching Negro History is Questionable." *Globe Democrat*, August 13, 1968, p. 6A.

"To Boycott or Not to Boycott? A Deadly Boomerang." *The Crisis*, 41 (September 1934), 259–60 and 274.

"Travelling Jim Crow." *The American Mercury*, 20 (August 1930), 423–32. Condensed in *Reader's Digest* (August 1930).

"A Treatise on Mulattoes." *The Crisis*, 44 (October 1937), 308–309.

"A Tribute to Caesar." *The Messenger*, 6 (July 1924), 225–26 and 231.

"Uncle Sam's Black Step-Child." *The American Mercury*, 29 (June 1933), 147–56.

"The Van Vechten Revolution." *Phylon*, 11 (Fourth Quarter 1930), 362–68.

"What the Negro Thinks of the South." *Negro Digest*, 2 (May 1945).

"What's Wrong with Negro Authors?" *Negro Digest,* 7 (May 1950), 3–7.

"What's Wrong with the NAACP?" *Negro Digest,* 4 (September 1947).

"When Black Weds White." *The Modern Monthly,* 5 (February 1934). Reprinted as lead article in the German magazine, *Die Auslese,* in June 1934.

"Why I Want to Stay in America." *Negro Digest,* 9 (June 1951), 52–56.

"Woman Palaver." *Globe* (March 1937).

"Woof." *Harlem,* 1 (November 1928), 17–20.

"The Yellow Peril: A One-Act Play." *The Messenger,* 7 (January 1925), 28–31.

"The Young Negro Co-Operative League." *The Crisis,* 39 (January 1932), 456 and 472.

SECONDARY SOURCES

1. Articles and Essays About Schuyler

"Author George S. Schuyler Dies at 82 in New York." *Jet,* 53 (September 29, 1977), 56.

Black No More: A Review. *Bookman,* 72 (February 1931), 7.

Black No More: A Review. *Boston Transcript,* February 21, 1931, p. 2.

Black No More: A Review. *Cleveland Open Shelf* (November 1931), 144.

Black No More: A Review. *The New Republic,* 65 (February 11, 1931), 362.

Black No More: A Review. *New York World,* January 16, 1931, p. 14.

Black No More: A Review. *Saturday Review of Literature,* 7 (May 2, 1931), 799.

Black No More: A Review. *Survey,* 66 (June 1, 1931), 290.

"Blame for the Riots as a Negro Writer Sees It." *U.S. News,* 63 (August 14, 1967), 10. Schuyler's views on Watts.

BONE, ROBERT A. *The Negro Novel in America.* New Haven: Yale University Press, 1958; rev. 1965. Bone views *Black No More* as an "assimilationist" instead of a "nationalistic" novel. A standard reference work.

BRAWLEY, BENJAMIN. *The Negro Genius: A New Appraisal of the Achievement of the American Negro in Literature and the Fine Arts.* New York: Dodd, Mead, 1937. Brief paragraphs on Schuyler. Helpful comments on the Harlem Renaissance.

BROWN, STERLING A. *The Negro in American Fiction.* Washington, D.C.: The Associates in Negro Folk Education, 1937; rpt. New York: Arno Press, 1969. Probably the most significant study of black letters prior to the 1960s. Good on the Harlem Renaissance. Brief paragraph on Schuyler's *Black No More.*

CALVIN, FLOYD J. "Schuyler's Book Dedicated to 'Pure' Whites." *The Pittsburgh Courier,* January 27, 1931, p. II–1. Favorable review of *Black No More.*

"Dark Slaves of Liberia." *The Pittsburgh Courier,* January 2, 1932 p. I–10.
Reprint of *The New York Evening Post* review of *Slaves Today.* A
favorable review.

DAVIS, ARTHUR P. "Black Satire," *Opportunity,* 9 (March 1931), 89–90.
Evenhanded analysis of *Black No More.*

————. *From The Dark Tower.* Washington: Howard University Press,
1974. Contains a chapter on Schuyler.

DU BOIS, W.E.B. "The Browsing Reader." *The Crisis,* 38 (January 1931),
16. Praises Schuyler's militancy and introduces the readers to "Black
Warriors."

————. "The Browsing Reader." *The Crisis,* 39 (March 1931), 100. An early
and favorable review of *Black No More.*

————. "The Browsing Reader." *The Crisis,* 41 (February 1932), 68–69.
Negative review of *Slaves Today.*

FISHER, RUDOLPH. Review of *Black No More. Books* (February 1931), 5.
Balanced review of the satire.

"George S. Schuyler, Iconoclast." *The Crisis,* 72 (October 1965), 484–85.
Editorial attacking Schuyler's outspoken comments on the Watts Riot
and Martin Luther King.

GLOSTER, HUGH. *Negro Fiction in the United States.* New York: Russell
and Russell, 1948. Positive statements about *Black No More* and *Slaves
Today.* Good survey of black authors through 1948.

GOODMAN, JR., GEORGE. "George S. Schuyler, Black Author." *New York
Times,* September 8, 1977, p. 40. Long, critically-balanced obituary.

HUGHES, CARL MILTON. *The Negro Novelist.* New York: Citadel Press,
1953. Brief comments on Schuyler's *Black No More,* but primary focus
on the 1940–1950 Negro novelists.

JANZ, JANHEINZ. *Neo-African Literature: A History of Black Writing.*
London: Faber and Faber, 1968; New York: Grove Press, 1969.
(Published by Faber and Faber as *A History of Neo-African Litera-
ture.*) Surveys African and black American literature. Praises Schuyler.

JONES, DEWEY R. A Review of *Slaves Today. Opportunity,* 10 (January
1932), 27. Favorable comments on the sociological implications of the
novel.

LARSON, CHARLES R. "Introduction." *Black No More.* New York: The
Macmillan Company, 1971. Develops the "urge to whiteness" theory
about Schuyler's satire; agrees essentially with Robert Bone's interpretation.

LEE, CARLETON L. A Review of *Black and Conservative. Negro History
Bulletin,* 30 (January 1967), 22–23. Somewhat unfavorable review of
Schuyler's autobiography.

"Liberia Today." *New York Times Book Review,* December 27, 1931, p. 9.
Reviews favorable and unfavorable aspects of *Slaves Today.*

LITTLEJOHN, DAVID. *Black on White: A Critical Survey of Writing by
American Negroes.* New York: Grossman Publishers, 1966. Survey of

prose and poetry, primarily twentieth century. Praises *Black No More*.

LOCKE, ALAIN. "We Turn to Prose: A Retrospective Review of the Literature of the Negro for 1931." *Opportunity*, 10 (February 1932), 43. Notes virtues and flaws of *Black No More*.

LOEB, WILLIAM. Correspondence with Michael W. Peplow. Letters dated January 16, 1974, and January 28, 1974.

MAYER, MARTIN. "Recordings." *Esquire*, 63 (March 1965), 52. "Meet the George Schuylers; America's Strangest Family." *Our World*, 6 (April 1951), 22–26. Nonliterature oriented, but nice background material on the family.

MENCKEN, H. L. "Check List of New Books." *The American Mercury*, 22 (April 1931), Brief, somewhat unfavorable review of *Black No More*.

———. "Check List of New Books." *The American Mercury*, 25 (February 1932). Critical review of *Slaves Today*.

———. "Editorial Notes." *The American Mercury*, 20 (August 1930). Mencken introduces young Schuyler and includes a brief autobiographical sketch that Schuyler submitted. Mencken's note also introduces "Travelling Jim Crow."

OVINGTON, MARY W. "Book Chat." *The Pittsburgh Courier*, February 6, 1932, p. II–2. Favorable review of *Slaves Today*, emphasizing its sociological significance.

PEPLOW, MICHAEL W. "The Black 'Picaro' in Schuyler's *Black No More*." *The Crisis*, 83 (January 1976), 7–10. Analysis of the *picaro*-trickster tradition in black literature and in *Black No More*.

———. "George Schuyler, Satirist: Rhetorical Devices in *Black No More*." *CLA Journal*, 18 (December 1974), 242–57. Analysis of the satiric devices Schuyler inherited and used in the novel.

PFEIFFER, JOHN. "Black American Speculative Literature: A Checklist." *Extrapolation: A Journal of Science Fiction and Fantasy*, 17 (December 1975), 35–43. Argues that *Black No More* is top-notch speculative fiction, "Swiftian" in nature, "with the underlying message, 'Black is beautiful.' "

RAYSON, ANN. "George Schuyler, Paradox Among 'Assimilationist' Writers," *Black American Literature Forum*, 12 (1978), 102–06.

REED, ISHMAEL. *Shrovetide in Old New Orleans*. New York: Doubleday and Company, Inc., 1978. Contains the October 1972 interview, "George S. Schuyler, Writer" that Steve Cannon and the author conducted; the interview was published in *Yardbird II* in 1973.

REILLY, JOHN M. "The Black Anti–Utopia," *Black American Literature Forum*, 12 (1978), 107–09.

"A Satire on Color." *New York Times Book Review*, February 1, 1931, p. 9. Balanced review of *Black No More*.

SCHRAUFNAGEL, NOEL. *From Apology to Protest: The Black American Novel*. Deland, Florida: Everette/Edwards, Inc., 1973, pp. 16–17. Brief mention of the historical significance of *Slaves Today*.

"Schuyler Calls for Historical Scientists." *Negro History Bulletin*, 18 (April 1955), 169–70. Article describes Schuyler's address to students on the contributions of black historians.

SCHUYLER, JOSEPHINE. "Black No More." *The Nation*, 132 (April 8, 1931), 132. Answers Dorothy Van Doren's comments about *Black No More*.

SMITH, WILLIAM GARDNER. "The Negro Writer: Pitfalls and Compensations," in *The Black American Writer*, vol. 1, edited by C. W. E. Bigsby. Deland, Florida: Everette/Edwards, Inc., 1969. Brief reference to *Black No More* as a "semi-classic" (p. 72).

TOLSON, MELVIN B. "George S. Schuyler." *The American Mercury*, 28 (March 1933), 373–74. The poet, then a young teacher, writes in praise of "Black Art," *Black No More*, and Schuyler's career in general to 1933.

VAN DOREN, DOROTHY. "Black, Alas, No More!" *The Nation*, 132 (February 25, 1931), 218–19. Argues that *Black No More* is "poor white satire."

WEST, HOLLIE I. "A Black, Biting John Bircher." *The Washington Post*, September 6, 1973, pp. C–1, C–8. Biographical sketch of Schuyler.

WHITLOW, ROGER. *Black American Literature: A Critical History*. Totowa, New Jersey: Littlefield, Adams and Company, 1974, pp. 96–100, 185. Brief yet objective report on Schuyler's career and major publications.

"Who's Who." *The Messenger*, 5 (June 1923), 748. Editorial introduces readers to George Schuyler, one of the young, intelligent, and "radical" New Negroes.

WINSLOW, H. F. "George S. Schuyler: Fainting Traveler." *Midwest Journal*, 5 (Summer 1953), 24–25.

2. Background Studies

ANDERSON, JERVIS. *A. Philip Randolph: A Biographical Portrait*. New York: Harcourt Brace Jovanovich, 1972. Significant study of one of the founders of *The Messenger* and of black history from the Harlem Renaissance to the 1970s.

ARNEZ, NANCY LEVI, and CLARA B. ANTHONY, "Contemporary Negro Humor as Social Satire," *Phylon*, 29 (1968), 339–46. Discussion of contemporary black satirists and their major themes.

BERGMAN, PETER M., and MORT N. BERGMAN, comps. *The Chronological History of the Negro in America*. New York: New American Library, 1969. A year-by-year compilation of significant events through 1968.

BONTEMPS, ARNA, ed. *The Harlem Renaissance Remembered*. New York: Dodd, Mead, 1972. Essays on major figures of the Harlem Renaissance. One of the better anthologies.

BROWN, STERLING A., ARTHUR P. DAVIS, and ULYSSES LEE, eds. *The Negro Caravan: Writings by American Negroes*. New York: Dryden,

1941; rpt. Arno Press, 1970. A milestone in black literature anthologies. Includes selections from *Black No More* and "Black Warriors."

COOKE, ALISTAIR, ed. *The Vintage Mencken.* New York: Vintage Books, 1956. Invaluable introductory essay and good collection of Mencken.

DORSON, RICHARD M., ed. *American Negro Folktales.* Greenwich, Conn.: Fawcett Publications, 1956, 1967. Valuable collection of black folktales.

DUNDES, ALAN, ed. *Mother Wit From the Laughing Barrel.* Englewood Cliffs: Prentice-Hall, 1973. Important collection of essays of black folklore.

FISHEL, LESLIE H., JR., and BENJAMIN QUARLES, eds. *The Black American: A Documentary History.* New York: Scott, Foresman, revised 1970. Standard collection of historical documents.

FORGUE, GUY J., ed. *Letters of H. L. Mencken.* New York: Alfred A. Knopf, 1961. Includes letters from Mencken to Schuyler.

GAYLE, ADDISON, JR., ed. *The Black Aesthetic.* Garden City, N.Y.: Doubleday and Company, 1971. Significant collection of essays by modern black scholars on a "black aesthetic" for the modern black artist or critic.

————, ed. *The Black Expression: Essays By and About Black Americans in the Creative Arts.* New York: David McKay, 1969. Another collection of significant essays on black literature, art, music.

"Harlem Renaissance Revisited." *Black World,* 20 (November 1970). Entire issue devoted to reappraisal of Harlem Renaissance and its major personalities.

HARRISON, JOHN M., and HARRY H. STEIN, eds. *Muckraking: Past, Present, and Future.* University Park: Pennsylvania State University Press, 1973. Collection of essays on the art of muckraking. Excellent background materials.

HIGHET, GILBERT. *The Anatomy of Satire.* Princeton: Princeton University Press, 1962. One of the standard studies of the art and techniques of satire.

HOLMAN, C. HUGH, comp. *A Handbook To Literature.* 3rd ed. New York: Odyssey Press, 1972. Revised and expanded version of the Thrall and Hibbard Handbook. Invaluable for students of literature.

HOPKINS, ERNEST J., comp. *The Ambrose Bierce Satanic Reader.* Garden City, N.Y.: Doubleday, 1968.

————. *The Complete Short Stories of Ambrose Bierce.* Garden City, N.Y.: Doubleday, 1970.

————. *The Enlarged Devil's Dictionary.* Garden City, N.Y.: Doubleday, 1967. The three volumes by Hopkins are the standard collection of Bierce's work. Each volume is accompanied by an informative introduction.

HUGGINS, NATHAN I. *Harlem Renaissance.* New York: Oxford University

Press, 1971. A modern and valuable critical overview of the era.

HUGHES, LANGSTON, ed. *The Book of Negro Humor*. New York: Dodd, Mead, 1966. Standard collection of folk and modern humor and satire.

HUGHES, LANGSTON, and ARNA BONTEMPS, eds. *The Book of Negro Folklore*. New York: Dodd, Mead, 1959. Invaluable collection of tales about High John de Conquer, Brer Rabbit, and other trickster-*picaros*.

LOCKE, ALAIN, ed. *The New Negro*. New York: Boni and Liveright, 1925; rpt. Atheneum, 1970. One of the most important Harlem Renaissance anthologies; includes the "The New Negro," by the editor. Indispensable resource.

MEIER, AUGUST, ELLIOTT RUDWICK, and FRANCIS L. BRODERICK, eds. *Black Protest Thought in the Twentieth Century, (formerly Negro Protest Thought in the Twentieth Century)*. 2nd ed. Indianapolis: Bobbs-Merrill, 1971. Standard resource work and perhaps the most comprehensive compilation of original texts and manifestos beginning with Booker T. Washington.

MINTZ, LAWRENCE. "Langston Hughes's Jesse B. Semple: The Urban Negro as Wise Fool." *Satire News Letter*, 7 (1969), 11–21. The urban trickster defined.

NOWER, JOYCE. "Foolin' Master." *Satire News Letter*, 7 (1969), 5–9. Important discussion of the trickster tradition in black folklore and literature.

OSOFSKY, GILBERT, ed. *Puttin' On Ole Massa*. New York: Harper and Row, 1969. The editor's introduction, especially "A Note on the Usefulness of Folklore," discusses the trickster role as revealed in the slave narratives collected in this text.

PEPLOW, MICHAEL W., and ARTHUR P. DAVIS, eds. *The New Negro Renaissance: An Anthology.* New York: Holt, Rinehart, 1975. Thematic arrangement. Includes excerpts from *Slaves Today* and two essays: "The Negro-Art Hokum" and "Our Greatest Gift to America."

ROSENBLATT, ROGER. *Black Fiction*. Cambridge, Mass.: Harvard University Press, 1974. Provides important background information on black trends and themes. The section on "Exceptional Laughter" analyzes black humor and satire.

SCHECHTER, WILLIAM. *The History of Negro Humor in America*. New York: Fleet Press, 1970. Brief passages on emergence of the rural and urban trickster.

SHAW, J. D. "William Cowper Brann." In *Brann the Iconoclast: A Collection of the Writings of W. C. Brann*. Waco, Texas: Herz Brothers, 1898. 2 vols.

SUTHERLAND, W. O. S. *The Art of the Satirist*. Austin: The University of Texas Press, 1965. Good discussion of the craft, technique, and history of satire.

TURNER, DARWIN T., comp. *Afro-American Writers*. New York: Appleton-Century-Crofts, 1970. Standard bibliography of black authors and background studies.

WAGNER, JEAN. *Black Poets of the United States: From Paul Laurence Dunbar to Langston Hughes.* Urbana: The University of Illinois Press, 1973. Translated by Kenneth Douglas from the original French edition of 1962. Carefully researched and documented study of black poetry.

WALDEN, DANIEL, ed., *W. E. B. Du Bois: The Crisis Writings.* New York: Fawcett, 1972. Important collection of Du Bois' editorials and columns, 1910–1934.

WICKS, ULRICH. "The Nature of Picaresque Narrative: A Modal Approach." *PMLA*, 89 (March 1974), 240–49. Catalogues major themes and methods of picaresque fiction.

Index